LATIMER STUDY 84

RESILIENCE

A Spiritual Project

BY KIRSTEN BIRKETT

The Latimer Trust

BV
4509.5
.B544
2016

Resilience: A Spiritual Project © Kirsten R Birkett 2015 All rights reserved.

ISBN 978-1-906327-43-9

Cover photo: Life in extreme conditions © macondos –fotolia.com

Scripture quotations are from the ESV® Bible (The Holy Bible, English Standard Version®), copyright © 2001 by Crossway, a publishing ministry of Good News Publishers. Used by permission. All rights reserved.

Published by the Latimer Trust August 2016

The Latimer Trust (formerly Latimer House, Oxford) is a conservative Evangelical research organisation within the Church of England, whose main aim is to promote the history and theology of Anglicanism as understood by those in the Reformed tradition. Interested readers are welcome to consult its website for further details of its many activities.

The Latimer Trust
London N14 4PS UK
Registered Charity: 1084337
Company Number: 4104465
Web: www.latimertrust.org
E-mail: administrator@latimertrust.org

Views expressed in works published by The Latimer Trust are those of the authors and do not necessarily represent the official position of The Latimer Trust.

CONTENTS

Preface

> *Therefore, having this ministry by the mercy of God, we do not lose heart* (2 Corinthians 4:1).

The trouble is, in ministry it can be only too easy to lose heart. Preaching the gospel will never be easy, as Paul explains in painful detail in the book of 2 Corinthians. Some will reject the message as the fragrance of death; even among those who receive it as the scent of life itself, many will fall into complaining and disagreement. While we may not all have to deal with floggings, beatings with rods or shipwreck as Paul did, we can certainly all resonate with:

> And, apart from other things, there is the daily pressure on me of my anxiety for all the churches. Who is weak, and I am not weak? Who is made to fall, and I am not indignant? (2 Corinthians 11:28-29).

There are any number of stresses in Christian ministry. Working in ministry will almost always mean dealing with people, and that is in itself stressful, even for ministers who love doing it. It involves listening to people with difficult lives, feeling their difficulties with them; there is second-hand stress as you worry about their problems as well as your own. In ministry, people do not generally come to you when things are going well or when their lives are wonderful. They come to the minister when they have a problem, when they have a crisis. It is inevitable that ministers will engage with a disproportionate amount of the suffering of the world.

Most full-time ministry positions will involve some level of leadership, and being in charge is in stressful. It is a high calling; there are expectations of a certain godliness of character as well as skilled ability. Most ministers will be acutely aware that they are not all they should be. Everyone judges the minister, and everyone has an opinion as to how the job could be done better. Any minister will be aware that you cannot please everyone; that is never the intention, anyway. Leadership puts people in a place of high visibility, and you will be under constant scrutiny. What is more, it is likely that those to whom you minister will assume that you are emotionally and spiritually fine. They will seek your help but they will rarely offer you help.

Christian ministry, especially in the evangelical world, is also likely to be very busy. There is always too much to do, and the feeling of being constantly on the run can create a constant low-level background of stress. Ministry is the kind of job that is never finished, because you are dealing with people. There will be a constant sense of incompletion. Moreover, given the way in which most churches run, it can be hard to know when work stops. The boundary of hours is blurred, and there may be no clear demarcation of when the day finishes.

Coping with stress in the secular world

The secular world is well aware of the problems of stress. Of recent decades a great deal of attention and research has been devoted to understanding what those who cope well with stress actually do; and, as a result, how to help others learn to do the same things. The psychological construct that has been developed to describe what secular researchers are looking for is resilience.

Resilience is not just about survival, but bouncing back more strongly. As such it is a central part of the general move within secular psychology towards what might be called a positive psychology; not just understanding how to treat problems, but understanding how to make healthy people even better. This is of interest to researchers not just as a theoretical effort to understand the human psyche, but is very relevant for those responsible for training people for stressful professions – the military, police, medicine and teaching are in the forefront of applied resilience research.

As created, embodied beings, who function in this world alongside others, it is useful for us to understand better how we are made; secular research, even that done from a very different ideological commitment from biblical Christianity, is useful to this end. Empirical results from studies that examine just how people respond to different situations and what in practice helps them respond better, is useful. It is in this spirit that I started researching the literature on resilience. My job, working in a theological college, is to help people prepare for a lifetime of Christian ministry. I was interested to find out, on a human level, what would help them survive and thrive in this stressful calling.

What the literature reveals, however, is that our created natures (not surprisingly) thrive on spiritual values. What fosters resilience, the qualities and strategies that resilient people demonstrate are things to do with meaning and morality and transcendence and relationships. The literature discusses things like religion and spirituality, altruism and belief in the good. Sometimes these ideas can sit oddly with the naturalistic, pluralistic framework of secular socio-scientific research. They do not sit at all oddly, however, within a Christian framework. It should not be surprising that what *works* is just that sort of lifestyle that God created us to have. It was, however, surprising just how strongly this comes through in an avowedly non-religious research setting.

What follows helps us to see just how our created, embodied natures respond to a spiritual life. Nothing will make Christian ministry *easy* in this fallen world, dealing with the sinful people that we all are. However we are blessed with resources that perhaps we take too lightly, and could be paying more attention to. We have a gracious God who has revealed truths about the world that make a difference to us – how we feel and how we cope, as well as how we believe and act. Most of all, unlike the secular world, we have a real hope that makes positive thinking entirely rational. As Paul said:

> So we do not lose heart. Though our outer self is wasting away, our inner self is being renewed day by day. For this light momentary affliction is preparing for us an eternal weight of glory beyond all comparison, as we look not to the things that are seen but to the things that are unseen. For the things that are seen are transient, but the things that are unseen are eternal (2 Corinthians 4:16-18).

1. Introduction

Christian ministry is a vocation which typically means working in a local church setting, either as the leader of the church or in some other capacity – youth and children's minister, families' minister, specialist ministries to women or men, and so on. Any of these positions will involve a lifetime of dealing with people, often in difficult situations, at times of key life events. These events often hold high levels of emotion – the joy of marriage, the grief of bereavement. Day to day, Christian ministry also involves running what can be a large and diverse organisation, given all the social and community activities that churches are commonly involved in. It requires intellectual acuity to exegete Scripture, prepare sermons and Bible studies, teach ethics and apologetics and answer questions of belief. It is a busy life, full of people work, often with low pay and in a world where the minister can be the focus of hostility. This is stressful.

Ministry is also a lifelong calling, and we would hope that those in full-time ministry have the wherewithal to deal with stress, and not be crushed by it. This is not just a matter of what is vaguely called 'work-life balance'. Our question is, are there any more definite qualities or practices that specifically help humans bounce back from difficult times? Is there anything we can concretely teach or recommend, beyond 'take a day off'? Is there anything we could learn about the human psyche that would tell us how to direct our efforts in the particular task of getting through, recovering from and learning from difficult times?

The problem of stress in ministry is a well-known one. There is a recognised published literature on burnout in Christian ministry.[1] It is a problem recognised by churches worldwide, and by the Church of England. There is also a large published literature on how theological

1 For instance, K J Randall, 'Burnout as a predictor of leaving Anglican parish ministry', *Review of Religious Research*, 46.1, 2004, pp 20-26; M Miner, S Sterland and M Dowson, 'Orientation to the demands of ministry: construct validity and relationship with burnout', *Review of Religious Research*, 50.4, 2009, pp 463-479; M H Miner, M Dowson and S Sterland, 'Ministry orientation and ministry outcomes: evaluation of a new multidimensional model of clergy burnout and job satisfaction', *Journal of Occupational and Organizational Psychology*, 83.1, 2010, pp 167-188.

education must adapt for 21st-century needs.[2] This is an issue that concerns churches and educational institutions; how to understand the world we live in, and how best to prepare students to minister within it. People in all brands of the Christian tradition are eager to find what will help ministers cope better with modern-day ministry.

How to cope with stress is also not a question limited to Christians. For the last few decades there has been an emerging research field into the human quality of resilience. It is a complex and diverse field, still developing, but so far has come to some fairly well established conclusions.

For instance, research into the idea of personal resilience has revealed that it is both a personality trait[3] and a process[4] that enables people to 'bounce back' from stressful situations. As a result of this research, various professions that involve potentially stressful situations – such as nursing, medicine and policing – have explored training employees in resilience. The results have been very positive.[5]

However, these two fields – the literature that recognises stress in Christian ministry, and the literature that studies resilience and how to get it – have not often overlapped. This is despite the fact that many interesting insights arise from resilience research, which might be adapted for Christian ministry. Psychological research on resilience, which has been carried out in a wide range of arenas, has identified certain qualities, strategies and activities that result in developing resilience in individuals. It asks the questions: what is resilience? What are its psychological components, and how does one obtain it?

---

2 Although on the whole this literature is not evangelical. For the British context, see for instance D Heywood, 'Educating ministers of character: building character into the learning process in ministerial formation', *Journal of Adult Theological Education,* 10.1, 2013, pp 4-24; M Fuller and K Fleming, 'Bridging a gap: a curriculum uniting competencies and theological disciplines', *Journal of Adult Theological Education* 2.2, 2005, pp 163-178; M Higton, *Vulnerable Learning: Thinking Theologically about Higher Education* (Cambridge: Grove Books, 2006).

3 T Hu, D Zhang and J Wang, 'A meta-analysis of the trait resilience and mental health', *Personality and Individual Differences,* 76, 2015, pp 18-27.

4 M Kent, M C Davis and J W Reich, 'Introduction' in *The Resilience Handbook: Approaches to Stress and Trauma* (New York and London: Routledge, 2014) pp xii-xix, p xii.

5 S S Chesak *et al*, 'Enhancing resilience among new nurses: feasibility and efficacy of a pilot intervention', *The Ochsner Journal,* 15.1, 2015, pp 38-44; L Walters *et al*, 'Exploring resilience in rural GP registrars – implications for training', *BMC Medical Education,* 15, 2015, pp 110-118; I Hesketh, J Ivy and J Smith, 'Keeping the Peelian Spirit: Resilience and Spirituality in Policing', *The Police Journal: Theory, Practice and Principles,* 87.3, 2014, pp 154-166.

Literature is also available on how professions which involve ongoing personal stress have applied this research in training programmes, to prepare their personnel for stressful lifestyles.

This short work presents the results of my reading over a wide range of articles and books on resilience. It surveys the research that has been done and what it recommends, with some conclusions about how we might apply these recommendations in ministry. There is a very large body of literature on resilience and how to achieve it, but to date very little of this has been applied to Christian ministry in particular. I came to the literature looking for ways to do just that.

This is not just a theoretical question for me. My job, as a lecturer at a theological college, is to help train people for a lifetime of ministry; as well as that, I have experienced stress-related depression in ministry myself. For me, Cognitive-Behavioural Therapy (CBT) was very successful. I have personally experienced, then, the reality of burnout as a result of stress, but also the real benefits that are available through good therapy, which were able to restore me to health. I have had the benefit of meeting many others who have similarly been helped by this kind of talking therapy that trains us to respond to problems differently by changing how we think about them.

While teaching Pastoral Care at Oak Hill College I thought a lot about what helps ministers, in practice, cope with the emotional burden of an intense job. This is a skill separate from, and in addition to, knowing how to cope with the emotional problems of others. Those going into ministry will certainly need an appreciation of the human person and development, with some understanding of psychology and how mind and emotions work, as well as practical counselling knowledge and skills. They will, in reality, need to know how to cope with church members who may have problems ranging from marriage breakup to depression to eating disorders, as well as the ordinary stresses of work, children (babies, toddlers, school-age, teenagers), bereavement, ageing and so on. This gives plenty of material to fill any course on pastoral care. As well as that, however, future ministers will need to have skills to deal with themselves, as human beings with their own emotional needs. We do not want ministers who will burn out; not only is that a terrible thing for the individual involved, it can be a loss of a great resource for the kingdom. There are training materials available; as well as the secular CBT material, the Christian counselling resources through organisations such as the Christian Counselling and Education Foundation provide very useful information.

Until recently, however, I was not aware of the literature on resilience. Although it covers a range of disciplines, it seems quite self-contained, with its own particular history which is not necessarily linked with literature on CBT or counselling more generally. When I started looking into it, I expected the advice to be almost entirely along the lines of the CBT techniques with which I was already familiar; that is, I expected the recommended training to be based on cognitive therapy, and to be entirely secular. I have been very surprised by the results of research, which openly recommend spirituality as part of developing resilience. It seems that my two concerns – training of minds to cope with stress, and training within a Christian spiritual context – overlap far more than I realised.

I did not set out to write about spiritual matters when I started researching resilience. I thought I was setting out to find out the best advice about psychological and lifestyle techniques that I would then seek to apply to a Christian ministry setting. I expected CBT-type practices, relaxation therapy, or some other secular physical or mental technique. I should have had more faith in my doctrine of creation. We are created to worship God and obediently live in self-sacrificial service to others; why should I be surprised that the tools he supplies to live that life, are shown experimentally to be effective? For that is what the literature shows. The developed qualities and habits that promote resilience are just those qualities that are part of living godly lives. The world may be fallen, but God's wisdom for living in it turns out to be what works.

2. Resilience research

Research over the last few decades has revealed, in detail, that humans on the individual or community level insist on thriving.[1] Even in the face of stress and disaster, humans have an astonishing capacity not just to survive, but to grow stronger. This has revolutionised the view of what distress and suffering does, whether that distress is chronic childhood abuse, a single extreme traumatic event or ongoing continuous stress. Resilience has been seen within a paradigm shift in the understanding of mental health,[2] from what might be called a 'disease model' to a 'resilience model'. While illnesses such as depression and post-traumatic stress disorder, and other physical and mental ailments, can and do occur as a result of trauma, such reactions are not inevitable. On the contrary, in some cases negative events lead to very positive outcomes. This leads researchers to conclude that 'healthy reactions to risk factors are the norm, not the unusual reaction for individuals and communities'; and 'resilience is a *distinct* process, independent of illness dimensions, and as such it has to be studied in its own right in terms of antecedent, process, and outcome variables.'[3]

The literature on resilience is vast, even though it is a relatively recent research topic. Valuable research which explores how resilience presents in different types of individuals has been carried out, but it is a young discipline in which some basic concepts are still in the process of being defined. There are many ways in which the literature could be divided, and any review can only be incomplete. We will first take a survey of the literature to get a sense of the range of areas and disciplines it covers. We will then look at some of the definitional debates, using the literature to understand better exactly what the concept of resilience is. This will give us both an idea of the scope of the field, and also an understanding of key ideas and concepts, and how

---

1 See, for instance, A E Skodol, 'The resilient personality', in *Handbook of Adult Resilience*, eds. J W Reich, A J Zautra and J S Hall (New York: Guilford Press, 2010) pp 112-125; M L Rutter *et al*, 'Specificity and heterogeneity in children's responses to profound institutional privation', *The British Journal of Psychiatry: The Journal of Mental Science*, 179, 2001, pp 97-103; M Rutter, 'Psychosocial resilience and protective mechanisms', *American Journal of Orthopsychiatry*, 57.3, 1987, pp 316-331.

2 T M Yates and A S Masten, 'Fostering the future: resilience theory and the practice of positive psychology', in *Positive Psychology in Practice*, eds. P A Linley and S Joseph (Hoboken, NJ: Wiley, 2004) pp 521-539.

3 J W Reich, A J Zautra and J S Hall, *Handbook of Adult Resilience*, p xii.

they are applied to different areas. Our ultimate goal is to discover the pertinent aspects of resilience that may be applied to Christian ministry.

2.1. *Disciplines involved in resilience research*

Articles on resilience cover a range of disciplines – psychology, psychopathology, sociology, biology and cognitive neuroscience – and topics – definitions, causes, applications – as well as a range of types of writing. There are a number of useful surveys or summary articles, which sum up aspects of resilience research to that point[4] or bring together the various psychological and social strengths which have been discovered to foster resilience.[5] The American Psychological Association website includes a large collection of papers on resilience as well as general survey articles.[6] A number of these also give accounts of the history of resilience as a concept and a research topic.[7] Over time, studies have covered recovery from chronic, long-term adversity in childhood as well as single traumatic events in adulthood.[8] Resilience seems to be a global phenomenon; not only do research papers cover populations from very different cultures, but research has been done specifically comparing resilience in children across different cultures.[9]

Articles from psychology or psychiatry, or the social sciences, tend to look into causes – what fosters, or creates, resilience. Again, some of these are general survey articles looking at a wide range of factors that

4 P A Atkinson, C R Martin and J Rankin, 'Resilience revisited', *Journal of Psychiatric and Mental Health Nursing*, 16.2, 2009, pp 137-145; E Grafton, B Gillespie and S Henderson, 'Resilience: the power within', *Oncology Nursing Forum*, 37.6, 2010, pp 698-705; D Fletcher and M Sarkar, 'Psychological resilience: a review and critique of definitions, concepts, and theory', *European Psychologist*, 18.1, 2013, pp 12-23; G Wu *et al*, 'Understanding resilience', *Frontiers in Behavioral Neuroscience*, 7, 2013, pp 10-25; K Tusaie and J Dyer, 'Resilience: a historical review of the construct', *Holistic Nursing Practice*, 18.1, 2004, pp 3-10; G A Bonanno, 'Uses and abuses of the resilience construct: loss, trauma, and health-related adversities', *Social Science and Medicine*, 74.5, 2012, pp 753-756.

5 B M Iacoviello and D S Charney, 'Psychosocial facets of resilience: implications for preventing posttrauma psychopathology, treating trauma survivors, and enhancing community resilience', *European Journal of Psychotraumatology*, 5, 2014, pp 1-10.

6 http://www.apa.org/helpcenter/road-resilience.aspx.

7 For instance, Atkinson, Martin and Rankin, 'Resilience revisited'.

8 Bonanno, 'Uses and abuses of the resilience construct'.

9 M Ungar, 'Resilience across cultures', *British Journal of Social Work*, 38.2, 2008, pp 218-235.

contribute to resilience: personal, experiential and biological.[10] More specifically, there has been research into the genes that indicate a tendency to resilience[11] and the brain science of resilience.[12] Some articles look in particular at the role of oxytocin, a neuropeptide. This chemical is already thought to increase interpersonal trust, reduce stress responses and protect against drug addiction and the negative effects of stress on health; more recently it has been argued that oxytocin increases resilience[13] – we all look forward to the day when it will be available in a tablet! Hein looks at the neuroscience of empathy, a strong element of resilience.[14]

A large part of the research looks at resilience as a trait or collection of traits; that is, the personality characteristics that correlate with having better resilience.[15] Boden *et al* emphasise the importance of regulating emotions in developing resilience.[16] Others look at resilience in relation

---

[10] For example, D Simeon *et al*, 'Factors associated with resilience in healthy adults', *Psychoneuroendocrinology*, 32.8, 2007, pp 1149-1152; A J Zautra, J S Hall and K E Murray, 'Resilience: a new definition of health for people and communities' in *Handbook of Adult Resilience*, pp 3-29.

[11] A Feder *et al*, 'Psychobiological mechanisms of resilience to stress' in *Handbook of Adult Resilience*, pp 35-54; K Lemery-Chalfant, 'Genes and environments: How they work together to promote resilience' in *Handbook of Adult Resilience*, pp 55-80.

[12] J Panksepp, 'Seeking and Loss in the Ancestral Genesis of Resilience, Depression, and Addiction' in *The Resilience Handbook: Approaches to Stress and Trauma* pp 1-14; M Tops *et al*, 'The roles of predictive and reactive biobehavioral programs in resilience' in *The Resilience Handbook: Approaches to Stress and Trauma*, pp 15-32; G B Raglan and J Schulkin, 'Introduction to allostasis and allostatic load' in *The Resilience Handbook: Approaches to Stress and Trauma*, pp 44-52.

[13] M Tops, F T Buisman-Pijlman and C S Carter, 'Oxytocin and attachment facilitate a shift from seeking novelty to recognizing and preferring familiarity' in *The Resilience Handbook: Approaches to Stress and Trauma*, pp 115-130; J L Frijling *et al*, 'Promoting resilience after trauma' in *The Resilience Handbook: Approaches to Stress and Trauma*, pp 299-308.

[14] G Hein, 'Empathy and resilience in a connected world' in *The Resilience Handbook: Approaches to Stress and Trauma*, pp 144-155.

[15] Hu, Zhang and Wang, 'A meta-analysis of the trait resilience and mental health'; J W Kim, H Lee and K Lee, 'Influence of temperament and character on resilience', *Comprehensive Psychiatry*, 54.7, 2013, pp 1105-1110; N Sarubin *et al*, 'Neuroticism and extraversion as mediators between positive/negative life events and resilience', *Personality and Individual Differences*, 82, 2015, pp 193-198; J S Robinson, C L Larson and S P Cahill, 'Relations between resilience, positive and negative emotionality, and symptoms of anxiety and depression', *Psychological Trauma: Theory, Research, Practice, and Policy*, 6, Suppl 1, 2014, pp S92-S98; Skodol, 'The resilient personality'.

[16] M T Boden *et al*, 'Responding to trauma and loss' in *The Resilience Handbook: Approaches to Stress and Trauma*, pp 86-99.

to happiness and positive emotions.[17] There are articles on resilience and music,[18] resilience and shame,[19] resilience and forgiveness,[20] resilience as a whole-life strategy,[21] and resilience and spirituality;[22] we will look in more detail at this area later.

2.2. *History of resilience research*

From the seventies onwards, insights on resilience came from research into survivors of abusive or violent childhoods. Attachment theory would suggest that severe childhood deprivation would leave children unable to flourish – unable to achieve at school and career, to maintain successful relationships, to live happy lives. However this was found to be not at all inevitable. Surprisingly, a percentage of children, despite terrible experiences, were able to achieve positive life outcomes. One study, for instance, followed a group of Hawaiian children from backgrounds of extreme deprivation and disadvantages, including poverty and fragmented families, who nonetheless went on to have relatively successful lives.[23] Another influential study on Romanian

---

17 W Lü *et al*, 'Resilience as a mediator between extraversion, neuroticism and happiness, PA and NA', *Personality and Individual Differences*, 63, 2014, pp 128-133; M A Cohn *et al*, 'Happiness unpacked: positive emotions increase life satisfaction by building resilience', *Emotion*, 9.3, 2009, pp 361-368; C E Waugh, 'The regulatory power of positive emotions in stress' in *The Resilience Handbook: Approaches to Stress and Trauma*, pp 73-85.

18 D A Hodges, 'Music as an agent of resilience' in *The Resilience Handbook: Approaches to Stress and Trauma*, pp 100-112.

19 K J V Van Vliet, 'Shame and resilience in adulthood: a grounded theory study', *Journal of Counseling Psychology*, 55.2, 2008, pp 233-245.

20 N G Wade, J R Tucker and M A Cornish, 'Forgiveness interventions and the promotion of resilience following interpersonal stress and trauma' in *The Resilience Handbook: Approaches to Stress and Trauma*, pp 256-269.

21 V Lankford, 'My whole life is Plan B: a psychological and practical approach to resilience', *Transactional Analysis Journal*, 42.1, 2012, pp 62-70.

22 C Gnanaprakash, 'Spirituality and resilience among post-graduate university students', *Journal of Health Management*, 15.3, 2013, pp 383-396; L K Manning, 'Navigating hardships in old age: exploring the relationship between spirituality and resilience in later life', *Qualitative Health Research*, 23.4, 2013, pp 568-575; M Khosravi and Z Nikmanesh, 'Relationship of spiritual intelligence with resilience and perceived stress', *Iranian Journal of Psychiatry and Behavioral Sciences*, 8.4, 2014, pp 52-56.

23 E E Werner and R S Smith, *Vulnerable but Invincible: A Longitudinal Study of Resilient Children and Youth* (New York: McGraw-Hill, 1981); also see N E Garmezy and M E Rutter, 'Stress, coping, and development in children', *Seminar on Stress and Coping in Children, 1979, Ctr for Advanced Study in the Behavioral Sciences* (Stanford, CA: Johns Hopkins University Press, 1983).

orphans adopted into Western families revealed that many of the children demonstrated substantial recovery in a number of areas. As the authors commented, 'It is sometimes supposed that lasting damage is inevitable after prolonged early institutional privation, but our results run counter to that view'.[24]

A new theory and a new research focus were needed to account for their success. The focus had been strongly on *pathology* – an illness model, which anticipates and looks for explanations of mental illness, seeking to identify what damage is done to children from difficult backgrounds. The focus was not entirely negative: after all, the purpose of identifying the damage was in order to provide the best possible treatment. However, with the discovery that many children seemed to avoid long-term damage, the focus moved to searching for strengths that explain the absence of expected mental illness; what was to account for their resilience?

At first, the search was primarily involved in identifying character traits that resilient children displayed, that were perhaps not there in the children who did not recover. Various traits were found and researched further. At the same time, researchers looked for external conditions that perhaps aided the development of resilience, such as particular types of social networks, parenting and families. This led to a gradual movement of discussion away from character traits to concentration on the *process* of developing resilience.

Resilience research, then, is part of a relatively new trend within mental health, that of strengths-based paradigms and positive psychology.[25] It is premised on the idea that not only are humans remarkably able to recover, but also the related idea that humans are able to change. Neither nature nor nurture is determinative in this view; humans are not fated to be moulded by either, but are able, indeed are highly suited, to change and grow stronger in the face of adversity.

2.3. *Resilience in specific groups*

Resilience has been found to be a relevant issue in a wide range of social groupings. There are many researchers who study resilience as it is evident, or might be encouraged, in specific groups. Early studies

---

24 Rutter *et al*, 'Specificity and heterogeneity in children's responses to profound institutional privation', pp 100-101.

25 M E Seligman, 'The optimistic child: a proven program to safeguard children against depression and build lifelong resilience', *Adolescence*, 32.126, 1997, p 502.

looked at survivors of deprived or abusive childhoods.[26] In the more recent literature there is much advice on how to help children and families.[27] Other articles advise how to teach resilience to adolescents,[28] and adolescents who have been sexually abused;[29] also young people who are victims of cyberbullying.[30] Bottrell studies resilience in relation to young people growing up in inner-city Sydney.[31] Work has been done on the impact of resilience, as well as the impact of early life stress, on patients with major depressive disorders.[32]

Older people have also been the focus of resilience research. Gallacher *et al* look at training older people in resilience to combat the effects of ill health.[33] The causes of resilience in middle-aged and older adults have also been studied in various ways.[34]

A growing amount of research is being done into resilience for teachers. In particular, researchers are interested in how to build resilience into young or beginning teachers, given the problem of

26 Werner and Smith, *Vulnerable but Invincible*; Garmezy and Rutter, 'Stress, coping, and development in children'.

27 M K Alvord and J J Grados, 'Enhancing resilience in children: a proactive approach', *Professional Psychology: Research and Practice*, 36.3, 2005, pp 238-245; D Gartrell and K B Cairone, 'Fostering resilience: teaching social-emotional skills', *YC Young Children*, 69.3, 2014, pp 92-93; J Clinton, 'Resilience and recovery', *International Journal of Children's Spirituality*, 13.3, 2008, pp 213-222.

28 P Cougar Hall and J H West, "Boundin': responding to life challenges with resilience', *Journal of School Health*, 82.4, 2012, pp 196-200; J S Davis, 'Building resilient students: three strategies for success', *Educational Horizons*, 92.2, 2013, pp 21-25; G Morrison and M Allen, 'Promoting student resilience in school contexts', *Theory Into Practice*, 46.2, 2007, pp 162-169.

29 J Williams and D Nelson-Gardell, 'Predicting resilience in sexually abused adolescents', *Child Abuse and Neglect*, 36.1, 2012, pp 53-63.

30 L H Papatraianou, D Levine and D West, 'Resilience in the face of cyberbullying: an ecological perspective on young people's experiences of online adversity', *Pastoral Care in Education*, 32.4, 2014, pp 264-283.

31 D Bottrell, 'Understanding 'marginal' perspectives: towards a social theory of resilience', *Qualitative Social Work*, 8.3, 2009, pp 321-339.

32 J Seok *et al*, 'Impact of early-life stress and resilience on patients with major depressive disorder', *Yonsei Medical Journal*, 53.6, 2012, pp 1093-1098.

33 J Gallacher *et al*, 'Resilience to health related adversity in older people', *Quality in Ageing and Older Adults*, 13.3, 2012, pp 197-204.

34 Manning, 'Navigating hardships in old age'; G M Wagnild and J A Collins, 'Assessing resilience', *Journal of Psychosocial Nursing and Mental Health Services*, 47.12, 2009, pp 28-33; W Randall *et al*, 'Narrative and resilience: A comparative analysis of how older adults story their lives', *Journal of Aging Studies*, 34, 2015, pp 155-161.

teacher retention.[35] The focus of such research is usually how to provide teachers with the individual resources to develop resilience, but Griffiths addresses resilience from an organisational/management perspective.[36] Resilience training is also considered particularly valuable for teachers in poor or deprived areas.[37]

Resilience training has been advised for social workers;[38] and resilience is seen as relevant to human resource management in the workplace.[39]

Another major area in which resilience concepts are being applied is the military. Specific training in resilience is recommended for active service men and women, as well as veterans.[40] American veterans of Afghanistan and Iraq showed a measurable improvement in recovery after resilience training.[41] Easterbrooks, Ginsburg and Lerner also studied what creates resilience in military children, who actually do remarkably well despite seemingly having many factors which might be

---

35 Le Cornu *et al*, 'Promoting early career teacher resilience: a framework for understanding and acting', *Teachers and Teaching*, 20.5, 2014, pp 530-546; J Y Hong, 'Why do some beginning teachers leave the school, and others stay? Understanding teacher resilience through psychological lenses', *Teachers and Teaching*, 18.4, 2012, pp 417-440; P A Doney, 'Fostering resilience: a necessary skill for teacher retention', *Journal of Science Teacher Education*, 24.4, 2013, pp 645-664; A Miller and S Gibbs, 'Teachers' resilience and well-being: a role for educational psychology', *Teachers and Teaching*, 20.5, 2014, pp 609-621; J Peters and J Pearce, 'Relationships and early career teacher resilience: a role for school principals', *Teachers and Teaching*, 18.2, 2012, pp 249-262; C Mansfield, S Beltman and A Price, "I'm coming back again!' The resilience process of early career teachers', *Teachers and Teaching*, 20.5, 2014, pp 547-567.

36 A Griffiths, 'Promoting resilience in schools: a view from occupational health psychology', *Teachers and Teaching*, 20.5, 2014, pp 655-666.

37 L Ebersöhn, 'Teacher resilience: theorizing resilience and poverty', *Teachers and Teaching*, 20.5, 2014, pp 568-594.

38 R Greene, C Galambos and Y Lee; 'Resilience theory: theoretical and professional conceptualizations', *Journal of Human Behavior in the Social Environment*, 8.4, 2004, pp 75-91.

39 E A Bardoel *et al*, 'Employee resilience: an emerging challenge for HRM', *Asia Pacific Journal of Human Resources*, 52.3, 2014, pp 279-297.

40 K H Thomas and S P Taylor, 'Beyond trauma treatment: mindfulness instruction in the training environment to prevent depression, lower suicide rates and improve resilience in the military and veteran communities', *Journal of Traumatic Stress Disorders and Treatment*, 4.2, 2015, pp np. Doi: http://dx.doi.org/10.4172/2324-8947.1000141.

41 W N Tenhula *et al*, 'Moving forward: A problem-solving training program to foster veteran resilience', *Professional Psychology: Research and Practice*, 45.6, 2014, pp 416-424.

expected to contribute to psychological trauma – parents in danger and spending long periods away, frequent moves and so on.[42]

Resilience training is also being applied in various aspects of medicine. Articles emphasise the need for nurses to be taught resilience in their training;[43] oncology nurses in particular have demonstrated positive results.[44] New nurses are also recommended resilience training.[45] Resilience training has been commended for Australian rural General Practitioners.[46] Loprinzi *et al* also study resilience training for cancer patients.[47]

Policing is another profession that involves stress, and potentially poor retention rates; it, too, has seen value in providing resilience training for employees.[48]

2.4. *Definitions of resilience*

> We all know perfectly well what resilience means until we listen to someone else try to define it.[49]

The original research into resilience involved individuals recovering from extreme circumstances. In most earlier (and some continuing) research, therefore, definitions of resilience emphasise this aspect: 'The ability to apparently recover from the extremes of trauma, deprivation, threat or stress is known as resilience'.[50] Scales that measure resilience have been based on such extremes of survival; for instance, the Connor-Davidson Resilience Scale (CD-RISC) was based in part on the qualities

---

42 M A Easterbrooks, K Ginsburg and R M Lerner, 'Resilience among military youth', *The Future of Children*, 23.2, 2013, pp 99-120, p 100.

43 H F Hodges, A C Keeley and E C Grier, 'Professional resilience, practice longevity, and Parse's theory for baccalaureate education', *The Journal of Nursing Education*, 44.12, 2005, pp 548-554.

44 Grafton, Gillespie and Henderson, 'Resilience'.

45 Chesak *et al*, 'Enhancing resilience among new nurses'.

46 Walters *et al*, 'Exploring resilience in rural GP registrars'.

47 C E Loprinzi, *et al*, 'Stress Management and Resilience Training (SMART) program to decrease stress and enhance resilience among breast cancer survivors: a pilot randomized clinical trial', *Clinical Breast Cancer*, 11.6, 2011, pp 364-368.

48 Hesketh, Ivy and Smith, 'Keeping the Peelian spirit'; B B Arnetz *et al*, 'Trauma resilience training for police: psychophysiological and performance effects', *Journal of Police and Criminal Psychology*, 24.1, 2009, pp 1-9.

49 Dr. George Vaillant, 1993; quoted in M J Davis, 'Defining Resilience', 1999, http://www.juvenilecouncil.gov/resilence/res_defin.html viewed 19/08/15.

50 Atkinson, Martin and Rankin, 'Resilience revisited', p 137.

displayed by Sir Ernest Shackleton that enabled him to survive his expedition to the Antarctic in 1912.[51]

How resilience is defined will affect where it is observed. Is it something in the person that is the cause of a good outcome, or is it a description of the outcome itself?[52] Is it observable before the stressful event, or only after? Both views are seen in the literature, as well as the composite idea that resilience is something created in the person or community as the stressful event (or events) is itself negotiated.

It would be easy to conclude, as some early researchers did, that resilience is shown by people who are resilient, and then seek to reduce the circularity of this definition by attempting to determine what personal qualities make up this characteristic of resilience. This is known as the 'trait' model of resilience, which informed a lot of research from the 70s onwards. What was difference between the successful survivors of trauma and the unsuccessful ones? Answers were looked for in the particular character traits displayed in the successes, and also in external characteristics of the survivors' lives. These were regarded as 'protective factors' that enable people to resist the negative effects of adversity and grow stronger in the face of it.[53]

Block and Block used the term 'ego resiliency' for those characteristics that 'keep the personality system within tenable bounds or permit the finding again of psychologically tenable adaptational modes'.[54] Ego-resiliency meant a kind of elasticity of the ego; an ability to adapt under 'environmental stress, uncertainty, conflict, or disequilibrium'.[55] Children with high ego-resiliency scores tended to be more empathic, able to cope with stress, bright, able to express emotion appropriately, self-accepting and novelty-seeking.[56] These were similar to the protective factors that Rutter described as 'influences that modify, ameliorate, or alter a person's response to some environmental hazard

---

51 K M Connor and J R Davidson, 'Development of a new resilience scale: the Connor-Davidson resilience scale (CD-RISC)', *Depression and Anxiety*, 18.2, 2003, pp 76-82, p 77.

52 Williams and Nelson-Gardell, 'Predicting resilience in sexually abused adolescents'.

53 Grafton, Gillespie and Henderson, 'Resilience'.

54 J H Block and J Block, 'The role of ego-control and ego-resiliency in the organization of behavior', in *Development of Cognition, Affect, and Social Relations: The Minnesota Symposia on Child Psychology*, ed. W Andrew Collins (New York and London: Psychology Press, 1980) pp 39-69, p 42.

55 Block and Block, 'The role of ego-control and ego-resiliency in the organization of behavior', p 48.

56 Block and Block, 'The role of ego-control and ego-resiliency in the organization of behavior', p 68.

that predisposes to a maladaptive outcome'.[57] Such influences did not necessarily just include personal characteristics of the resilient person, but might also be characteristics of their environment: loving family, social networks and so on.[58] The basic definition remains, nonetheless, that resilience is a collection of describable characteristics found by studying the resilient person.

However, the 'trait' model was not the only way in which resilience was understood. Some researchers even explicitly rejected it, seeing the 'trait' model as too restrictive.

> Resilience is neither a personal attribute or trait, nor something that is present in a young person's environment. Rather, resilience comes from interactions between people and their environments as part of a "dynamic developmental system".[59]

It is not that the individual or the situation is irrelevant or arbitrary; they may display characteristics that 'boost' resilience, but they are not included in the concept of resilience itself. Similarly, Papatraianou, Levine and West give their 'ecological' theory of resilience that in the face of adversity individuals can find their way to health-sustaining resources including opportunities to experience feelings of wellbeing.[60]

This definition sees resilience as a dynamic process. It describes the pattern of facing adversity and adapting, either to come back to equilibrium – 'an ability to bounce back from negative emotional experiences and flexibly adapt to the changing environment'[61] – or to come to a place of even greater strength than before – 'the capacity to maintain or recover higher well-being in the face of life adversity'.[62] In

---

57 M Rutter, 'Resilience in the face of adversity. Protective factors and resistance to psychiatric disorder', *The British Journal of Psychiatry: The Journal of Mental Science*, 147, 1985, pp 598-611, p 600.

58 M Rutter, 'Psychosocial resilience and protective mechanisms', *American Journal of Orthopsychiatry*, 57.3, 1987, pp 316-331.

59 Easterbrooks, Ginsburg and Lerner, 'Resilience among military youth', p 100.

60 Papatraianou, Levine and West, 'Resilience in the face of cyberbullying'.

61 Lü *et al*, 'Resilience as a mediator between extraversion, neuroticism and happiness, PA and NA', p 129; see also Simeon *et al*, 'Factors associated with resilience in healthy adults'; A M Pidgeon, L Ford and F Klaassen, 'Evaluating the effectiveness of enhancing resilience in human service professionals using a retreat-based Mindfulness with Metta Training Program: a randomised control trial', *Psychology, Health and Medicine*, 19.3, 2014, pp 355-364.

62 Lü *et al*, 'Resilience as a mediator between extraversion, neuroticism and happiness, PA and NA', p 129; see also Zautra, Hall and Murray, 'Resilience'; Loprinzi, *et al*, 'Stress Management and Resilience Training (SMART) program to decrease stress and enhance resilience among breast cancer survivors'.

this sense, resilience is the process itself, resulting in adaptation despite experiencing adversity.[63] The personality characteristics may still be there, but the resilience is displayed not by the possession of these characteristics, but by the process of using such internal (and external) resources in order to recover. This moves resilience from something that people just 'have' (or do not have) to something that can be taught, and learned.[64]

This desire to see resilience as a learnable skill is reflected in the American Psychological Association's website: 'Resilience is not a trait that people either have or do not have. It involves behaviors, thoughts and actions that can be learned and developed in anyone'.[65] Alvord and Grados, who define resilience broadly as 'those skills, attributes, and abilities that enable individuals to adapt to hardships, difficulties, and challenges',[66] describe it both as something that can be learned and being to some extent biologically determined.

The emphasis on resilience as process rather than personality also brought to the fore the importance of adversity; resilience is not something that is developed in a vacuum. It requires the tempering force of adversity for it to be displayed. Doney insists that 'resilience is not an innate personality trait, but rather a process that is both internal and external resulting from positive adaption to adversity'.[67] Resilience is built when stress is applied and protective factors are accessed. Both stressors and protective factors are necessary. This research assumes that life will be tough.

Indeed, says Tusaie, resilience is to be understood in relation to stress, and a comprehensive range of factors. It is both personal and contextual. 'Although each individual possesses the potential for resilience, an interplay between the individual and the broader environment is responsible for the level of resilience.'[68] Risk factors could be multiple life stressors, a single traumatic event, or cumulative stress from a number of individual and environmental factors. It might be risk to an entire group – such as children in poverty – or individually – an experience of trauma or an adverse event. 'The balance between

---

63 B M Gillespie *et al*, 'Resilience in the operating room: developing and testing of a resilience model', *Journal of Advanced Nursing*, 59.4, 2007, pp 427-438.

64 Grafton, Gillespie and Henderson, 'Resilience'.

65 American Psychological Association, 'The road to resilience: What is resilience?', 2016, http://www.apa.org/helpcenter/road-resilience.aspx

66 Alvord and Grados, 'Enhancing resilience in children', p 238.

67 Doney, 'Fostering resilience', p 653; see also Fletcher and Sarkar, 'Psychological resilience'.

68 Tusaie and Dyer, 'Resilience', p 3.

risk and protective factors is a dynamic process.'[69] Protective factors can also be individual or environmental. There are many forms of stress and adversity but there is reason for optimism about intervention programs to promote health and prevent illness.

Taking the general applicability of resilience even further, some researchers have described resilience in even more comprehensive terms, as something that is innate to all humans, and which can even be thought of in terms of a 'life force' or something similar.[70] At this point, resilience becomes something obviously desirable but almost too general and vague to be a useful concept.

A review of the literature, and the trends that have developed in resilience research, lead us to a comprehensive and complex construct. As Gallacher *et al* comment, although several scales have been developed to assess resilience, it is unlikely that there is a specific 'resilience' trait.[71] A more plausible model is a process involving motivational, practical and social competencies that promote emotional wellbeing and physical health. This process may come more sharply into focus in response to acute adversities or crises (such as incident disease, unemployment, bereavement or extreme environmental events), but is also implicated in responding to chronic adversities such as daily hassles, and the on-going pressures of life including chronic disease.

Being such a broad construct, it can be difficult to pin down. Some researchers lament that the field is hampered, due to a 'lack of a uniform operational definition for resilience and a corresponding methodology for studying it'.[72] Fletcher and Sarkar list nine different definitions of resilience, with different experimental emphases and seventeen models or theories of resilience.[73] Aranda and Hart in turn list 13 definitions.[74] By 2012, Michael Rutter, one of the original researchers in the 'trait' model, had come to a much more complex definition: 'reduced vulnerability to environmental risk experiences, the overcoming of a stress or adversity, or a relatively good outcome despite

69 Tusaie and Dyer, 'Resilience', p 4.

70 See Grafton, Gillespie and Henderson, 'Resilience'.

71 J Gallacher *et al*, 'Resilience to health related adversity in older people', *Quality in Ageing and Older Adults*, 13.3, 2012, pp 197-204.

72 Hu, Zhang and Wang, 'A meta-analysis of the trait resilience and mental health', p 18.

73 Fletcher and Sarkar, 'Psychological resilience', pp 13, 18.

74 K Aranda and A Hart, 'Resilient moves: tinkering with practice theory to generate new ways of thinking about using resilience', *Health*, 19.4, 2015, pp 355-371, p 358.

risk experiences'.[75] This is similar to Lee *et al* who see resilience as 'a multidimensional variable consisting of psychological and dispositional attributes, such as competence, external support systems, and personal structure'.[76] We find ourselves with multiple-clause sentences to try to include all these aspects:

> In the context of exposure to significant adversity, whether psychological, environmental, or both, resilience is both the capacity of individuals to navigate their way to health-sustaining resources, including opportunities to experience feelings of well-being, and a condition of the individual's family, community and culture to provide these health resources and experiences in culturally meaningful ways.[77]

The important practical implication is that, if resilience can be learned, then people can be trained against future stress.

---

75 M Rutter, 'Resilience as a dynamic concept', *Development and Psychopathology*, 24.2, 2012, pp 335-344, p 336.

76 J H Lee *et al*, 'Resilience: a meta-analytic approach', *Journal of Counseling and Development*, 91.3, 2013, pp 269-279, p 269.

77 Ungar, 'Resilience across cultures', p 225.

3. How does one acquire resilience?

How one defines resilience, of course, has an immediate effect on what one thinks it consists of, and therefore how one can get it. In some ways, determining this is a somewhat easier task than trying to pin down a definition. For instance, a trait definition will give a list of character traits that comprise resilience; but process definitions also include personal traits, that are part of the resources accessed during the process of acquiring resilience. There are a cluster of personal qualities that appear frequently in the literature as being the basis of resilience.

3.1. *Positive outlook*

A number of characteristics which might be roughly grouped together as 'positive outlook' have been identified as central to developing resilience. For instance, Grafton, Gillespie and Henderson write of hardiness, coping, self-efficacy, optimism, patience, tolerance, faith, adaptability, self-esteem, and a sense of humour, as well as social support and cognitive ability.[1] Hope and self-efficacy have been demonstrated as key factors.[2]

Proactive orientations, taking initiative in one's own life and believing in one's own effectiveness, is a primary characteristic defining resilience. It includes feeling that one can have an impact on the situation rather than just be passive, and being hopeful about the future, confident in ability to surmount obstacles. 'One of the most fundamental protective factors is success in developing self-regulation or self-control'.[3] Fletcher and Sarkar identify an easy temperament, good self-esteem, planning skills, and a supportive environment inside and outside the family.[4]

Indeed, despite the move away from a trait definition, research still suggests that personality type has a strong effect on resilience. Low neuroticism and high extraversion are fairly reliable predictors of resilience. Some psychologists still insist that a person's individual characteristics are more related to resilience than interpersonal

---

1 Grafton, Gillespie and Henderson, 'Resilience'.
2 Gillespie et al, 'Resilience in the operating room'.
3 Alvord and Grados, 'Enhancing resilience in children', p 240.
4 Fletcher and Sarkar, 'Psychological resilience'.

relationships, environmental factors, and maltreatment.[5] Lü *et al* write that childhood positive attitude, and extraversion, predict a resilient adult – however this is not to condemn non-extraverts to low resilience, as they also think individuals can learn resilience even if they are not extravert.[6]

This fits with what Robinson, Larson and Cahill conclude: the biggest variance in resilience between individuals is associated with positive characteristics rather than negative ones.[7] The empirical support for adaptive function of positive emotions is growing. Positive emotions, it seems, promote flexibility in thinking and problem solving, counteract the physiological effects of negative emotions, facilitate adaptive coping, build psychological and social resources, and enduring well-being, and are a basic building block of resilience.[8]

Wagnild and Collins, who researched middle-aged and older adults, associate resilience with

> inner strength, competence, optimism, flexibility, and the ability to cope effectively when faced with adversity ... forgiveness, morale, purpose in life, sense of coherence, self-transcendence and self-efficacy.[9]

Mindfulness is sometimes recommended as a therapy to promote resilience, as well as positive emotions: moment-to-moment awareness of bodily activities, feelings, emotions or sensation and discarding any distracting thoughts.[10]

3.2. *Self-efficacy*

It is worth bringing out one characteristic that occurs repeatedly: self-efficacy. It can be defined as a belief in one's own abilities to manage

---

5 Sarubin *et al*, 'Neuroticism and extraversion as mediators'.

6 Lü *et al*, 'Resilience as a mediator between extraversion, neuroticism and happiness, PA and NA'.

7 Robinson, Larson and Cahill, 'Relations between resilience, positive and negative emotionality, and symptoms of anxiety and depression'.

8 A D Ong, C Bergeman and S Chow, 'Positive emotions as a basic building block of resilience in adulthood', in *Handbook of Adult Resilience*, eds. J W Reich, A J Zautra and J S Hall, pp 81-93.

9 Wagnild and Collins, 'Assessing resilience', p 29.

10 Thomas and Taylor, 'Beyond Trauma Treatment'; Pidgeon, Ford and Klaassen, 'Evaluating the effectiveness of enhancing resilience in human service professionals using a retreat-based Mindfulness with Metta Training Program'; see also Mark Williams and Danny Penman, *Mindfulness: a Practical Guide to Finding Peace in a Frantic World* (London: Piatkus, 2011) and Michael Chaskalson, *Mindfulness in Eight Weeks* (London: HarperThorsons, 2014).

life's challenges and situations effectively.[11] It is in this sense the opposite of neuroticism, which involves seeing the world as threatening, problematic and distressing, and viewing oneself as vulnerable. Also, '[s]elf-understanding gives resilient people a strong sense of personal identity; they see themselves as coherent personalities with meaning and purpose to their lives'.[12] There often is also a spiritual side to the resilient person. These views boil down to four prototypical groups of traits: confident optimism, productive activity, insight and warmth, and skilled expressiveness.[13]

Self-efficacy is also strongly correlated with resilience in studies of teachers.[14] In this research, external influences, environment and actual ability or skill were not found to directly affect performance; they are filtered through one's beliefs about one's capabilities. Motivation, affective states and actions are based more on what they believe than on what is objectively true. 'This is because self-efficacy beliefs help determine what individuals do with the knowledge and skills they have'.[15] Also,

> [i]t seems that teachers who have a stronger sense of efficacy perceive difficulties as challenges rather than threats, and thus invest their effort in the face of adversities and direct their efforts in resolving problems.[16]

Those with a low sense of efficacy believe there is little they can do, so exert less effort and do not persevere.

3.3. *External factors*

As well as emotional outlook, certain external factors seem to have an impact on resilience. For instance, external influences that help children develop resilience are competent parents, friendships, support networks and good schools.[17] However, not all agree that external environment is significant for resilience. Lee *et al* ranked factors that affect resilience, finding the protective factors the most influential: life satisfaction, optimism, positive affect, self-efficacy, self-esteem and social support.

---

11 Skodol, 'The resilient personality'.
12 Skodol, 'The resilient personality', pp 114-5.
13 Skodol, 'The resilient personality', p 115.
14 Hong, 'Why do some beginning teachers leave the school, and others stay?'
15 Hong, 'Why do some beginning teachers leave the school, and others stay?', p 420.
16 Hong, 'Why do some beginning teachers leave the school, and others stay?, p 420.
17 Papatraianou, Levine and West, 'Resilience in the face of cyberbullying'.

Certain risk factors had a medium effect: depressive symptoms, anxiety-related impairments, high levels of stress. Demographic factors, in their research, showed the lowest effect.[18]

3.4. Meaning and morality

Iacoviello and Charney identify cognitive flexibility as an important part of developing resilience; being able to reappraise one's perception and experience of a traumatic situation. 'Reappraisal can also involve an effort to find meaning and positive outcomes ... acknowledging that experiences with stress, or even trauma, can provide opportunities for growth'.[19] They noted that resilient people display active coping skills and maintained a social support network: 'Considerable emotional strength accrues from close relationships with people and even organizations'.[20] They were active rather than passive, not letting themselves be consumed by fear. Physical activity and a personal moral compass were also significant: 'Holding a set of core beliefs that are positive about oneself and one's role in one's world, and that few things can shatter'.[21] Altruism was seen as a key part of resilience: 'Altruistic behaviour ... can also contribute to perceived meaning and purpose in life', another key part of resilience; specifically, 'faith in conjunction with religion or spirituality'.[22] Forgiveness is also an important attribute to develop in order to foster resilience.[23]

Wu *et al* also write of cognitive reappraisal in resilience: the ability to monitor and assess negative thoughts and replace them with more positive ones – 'finding the silver lining', or finding a meaning in life events.[24] This is also known as cognitive flexibility or cognitive reframing. This is connected with active coping, using behavioural or psychological techniques to reduce or overcome stress, rather than avoidant coping (emotional or behavioural withdrawal, or things such as alcohol use). This accords with researchers who discovered that the temperament traits of persistence and low harm avoidance (roughly,

---

18 Lee *et al*, 'Resilience: a meta-analytic approach'.

19 Iacoviello and Charney, 'Psychosocial facets of resilience', p 3.

20 Iacoviello and Charney, 'Psychosocial facets of resilience', p 3.

21 Iacoviello and Charney, 'Psychosocial facets of resilience', p 4.

22 Iacoviello and Charney, 'Psychosocial facets of resilience', p 4.

23 Wade, Tucker and Cornish, 'Forgiveness interventions and the promotion of resilience'.

24 Wu *et al*, 'Understanding resilience'.

tackling problems rather than avoiding them) are strongly correlated with resilience.[25]

Wu *et al* also stress that it helps if people have a moral compass: 'The existence of a moral compass or an internal belief system guiding values and ethics is commonly shared among resilient individuals.'[26]

3.5. *A combination of internal traits and external environment*

The majority of researchers see resilience as developing when internal and external factors are brought together. Problem-solving abilities, empathy, self-efficacy, optimism and family are identified by Kim, Lee and Lee as qualities that support and strengthen a person's resilience, because they enable a person to become more active and to utilise socially available strategies for overcoming risk factors.[27] Humour is a form of active coping as it alleviates tension and also attracts social support. Physical exercise affects neurobiological factors of resilience in animal and human studies; also prosocial behaviour and altruism are beneficial.[28]

Tusaie and Dyer list cognitive factors such as optimism, intelligence, creativity, humour, belief system that provides existential meaning, a cohesive life narrative, and appreciation of the uniqueness of oneself, and competencies including coping strategies, social skills, education abilities, and above-average memory. Social support, by which is meant not just the number or function of social relationships but also the perception of the support, is also listed as important.[29] Similarly, Easterbrooks, Ginsburg and Lerner list intelligence and cognitive flexibility; positive regulation and expression of emotion; an internal locus of control; personal agency and self-regulation; a sense of humour; and easy or sociable temperament; optimism and good health, which they see as not just defining features of an individual, but depending greatly on family, social and community environment.[30]

Atkinson, Martin and Rankin see significant factors in four patterns: dispositional, relational, situational and philosophical. Their cited factors include good health, intelligence, easy-going temperament,

---

[25] Kim, Lee and Lee, 'Influence of temperament and character on resilience'.
[26] Wu *et al*, 'Understanding resilience', p. 7.
[27] Kim, Lee and Lee, 'Influence of temperament and character on resilience'.
[28] Wu *et al*, 'Understanding resilience'.
[29] Tusaie and Dyer, 'Resilience'.
[30] Easterbrooks, Ginsburg and Lerner, 'Resilience among military youth'.

sociability, self-efficacy, confidence, optimism, hope, social support, problem-solving ability, internal locus of control, appraisal skills, flexibility in goal setting and the ability to mobilise resources.[31] Cross-cultural research into resilience has identified certain universal characteristics in resilient individuals, including affiliation with a religious organisation, toleration of different ideologies, self-betterment, having a life philosophy, cultural/spiritual identification, being culturally grounded ('knowing where you came from'); good relationships; individual qualities such as assertiveness, problem-solving ability, a sense of control, being able to live with uncertainty, self-awareness, perceived social support, optimism, empathy, having goals, a balance between independence and dependence, good attitude to alcohol, a sense of humour, sense of duty.[32] In children, intelligence, success at making friends, and ability to regulate behaviour have been identified as internal strengths that enhance resilience.[33]

As well, it is worth remembering that resilience comes from facing adversity.[34] Resilience research is about how people respond to stressors of all different sorts, and so how they can learn to respond to it better in the future.

3.6. *Problems with a focus on resilience*

Resilience would seem to be the answer to all our problems. Indeed, when we see a description of the resilient person as described by Skodol, she seems to be superwoman: goal-directed, industrious and productive, full of positive emotions, motivated to achieve and be successful in diverse aspects of life, with social poise and presence, curiosity, competence, insight and humour[35] – what hope is there for the rest of us! This is one of the potential downsides of focussing on resilience; it becomes an almost impossible ideal. This is unfortunate, since the point is to help people use the resources they already have to face the distress that will inevitably occur in life.

Atkinson, Martin and Rankin also identify other risks of this research, namely faddism, 'magic bullet' thinking, and blaming the victim for poor results.[36] Aranda and Hart add in this vein that although

---

31 Atkinson, Martin and Rankin, 'Resilience revisited', p 142.

32 Ungar, 'Resilience across cultures'.

33 Alvord and Grados, 'Enhancing resilience in children'.

34 Fletcher and Sarkar, 'Psychological resilience'; Doney, 'Fostering resilience'.

35 Skodol, 'The resilient personality', p 115.

36 Atkinson, Martin and Rankin, 'Resilience revisited'.

resilience research seems to 'resonate with the immediate concerns of everyday practice and lived experiences or struggles with disability, disadvantage or exclusion', it has a 'potential to be complicit with neoliberal imperatives of personal rather than social or structural change'.[37] If individuals are not thriving, it's not their disadvantage that's the problem, it's their own fault – they're just not being resilient enough.

We do not want to emphasise resilience as the cure-all, whether it is as a response to historic disadvantage or day-to-day stress. Sometimes people just need to recognise that they are tired and need time out. Some of the ways in which people display resilience are not right for others. A 'resilient' response to trauma and loss, for instance, is defined as one that sees 'modest to no disruption in normal functioning' – this is simply not how most people grieve, even if in the end they recover.[38] Sometimes we need to just stop and weep. Also, some see the emphasis on positive psychology as taking the focus away from the achievements of those in real distress.[39] Anecdotal evidence suggests that resilience training can be insensitively imposed; one nurse I spoke to talked scathingly of compulsory resilience training, scheduled in the middle of a busy shift, with no corresponding reduction in the number of tasks she was required to complete during that shift – the resilience training itself was significantly contributing to the stress of the job!

However, if we keep resilience in perspective, as ways of helping healthy people stay healthy and of helping ill people recover, it seems to be an extremely useful construct. Human beings are resilient – we could have hardly survived this long otherwise.

---

37 Aranda, K. and Hart, A., 'Resilient moves: Tinkering with practice theory to generate new ways of thinking about using resilience', *Health*, 19.4, 2015, pp 355-371.

38 Boden *et al*, 'Responding to trauma and loss'.

39 M Rutter, 'Resilience as a dynamic concept', *Development and psychopathology*, 24.2, 2012, pp 335-344, p 336.

4. Resilience and Christian spirituality

4.1. *Resilience research in Christian ministry*

As we have seen, resilience is a concept that is being researched over the whole of human experience; in different cultures, different professions, different ages and from a range of different perspectives. Christian ministry would seem to be a natural place to apply such research. It is a vocation that involves work with people, often in difficult life situations. It involves counselling and direct involvement in life's struggles (hospital visits, funerals, practical help in illness and bereavement). It frequently involves organising large events and large groups of people, working with volunteers. It requires intellectual engagement with big ideas, and teaching on multiple levels. It will frequently involve working with all ages from toddlers to teenagers to adults to the elderly, requiring an ability to engage with others' interests and life stages at all levels. It will involve dealing with opposition and strong emotions as well as times of joy and satisfaction. It has the potential to be highly stressful, lonely and difficult without immediate reward. In other words, it is a field where resilience in the face of ongoing stress would be a highly desirable quality to develop.

Given this, it is surprising that the immense literature on resilience does not include much that is specifically directed towards the pastoral ministry. In fact, there is almost *nothing* applying resilience research to the vocation of Christian ministry. There are a few books in the general area from a more Catholic or liberal point of view,[1] and some evangelical,[2] but virtually no research literature.

This is surprising on a number of levels.

---

1 C S Titus, *Resilience and the Virtue of Fortitude: Aquinas in Dialogue with the Psychosocial Sciences*, (Washington DC: The Catholic University of America Press, 2006); J Allain-Chapman, *Resilient Pastors: The Role of Adversity in Healing and Growth* (London: SPCK, 2012).

2 Bob Burns and Tasha D Chapman, *Resilient Ministry: What Pastors Told Us About Surviving and Thriving* (Downers Grove, IL: IVP, 2013 – sadly out of print); and Jay Burns, *Resilience: A Biblical, Gospel-Centred Guide to Long-Term Fruitfulness and Joy in the Service of Jesus Christ* (only available on Kindle, 2015); Mark A Searby, *The Resilient Pastor: Ten Principles for Developing Pastoral Resilience* (Eugene, Oregon: Resource Publications, 2015).

4.2. *Ministry and burnout*

It is not as if the stressfulness of ministry has not been recognised. There is a small but important literature about burnout in ministry – the experience of emotional exhaustion, depersonalisation and lacking a sense of personal accomplishment, which can lead to physical and/or mental illness (such as depression). Miner, Sterland and Dowson write of the characteristics of ministry that have been identified in research as primary correlates of burnout:

> [H]eavy workloads and time pressures, together constituting work overload; role conflict; role ambiguity; problems relating to autonomy; lack of social support; and conflicts concerning organizational values.[3]

Their study considers the additional pressure of societal secularisation, with its related challenged to clergy authority and undermining of significance.[4] Evers and Tomic also refer to secularisation as a pressure; as well as this, they add that the ageing population increases pastoral care responsibilities.[5] Burnout is a predictor of leaving the ministry,[6] and so is costly to religious organisations as well as to ministers and their families.

However there seems to be very little written about resilience and clergy, even though at least one study recognises that transcendent spirituality – a feeling of relationship with the Divine, the ability to lose oneself in prayer or meditation – makes burnout less likely.[7] Also, burnout is moderated by having a sense of self as separate from the role, and a collaborative conflict management style.[8] These seem very close to key factors cited by research as promoting resilience.

4.3. *Resilience and spirituality*

The second reason why it is surprising that there is not more written about resilience in Christian ministry is that the literature *does* include a

3 M Miner, S Sterland and M Dowson, 'Orientation to the demands of ministry', p 464.

4 M H Miner, M Dowson and S Sterland, 'Ministry orientation and ministry outcomes'.

5 W Evers and W Tomic, 'Burnout among Dutch Reformed pastors', *Journal of Psychology and Theology*, 31.4, 2003, pp 329-338.

6 Randall, 'Burnout as a predictor of leaving Anglican parish ministry'.

7 J Golden *et al*, 'Spirituality and burnout: an incremental validity study', *Journal of Psychology and Theology*, 32.2, 2004, pp 115-125.

8 R S Beebe, 'Predicting burnout, conflict management style, and turnover among clergy', *Journal of Career Assessment*, 15.2, 2007, pp 257-275

great deal about the importance of spirituality and religious affiliation in promoting resilience.

Empirical studies demonstrate that spirituality leads to a heightened ability to cope with stress. It helps with both problem-focused coping styles – dealing with difficulty by fixing the problem, which men tend to favour, and also emotion-focused coping styles – handling feelings of distress well, which women tend to favour.[9]

> The findings revealed that spirituality mediates the choice of emotional regulation strategies by altering the individual's cognitive appraisal process, such that individuals are able to reframe or reinterpret adverse experiences.[10]

In other words, spirituality is a means by which individuals access the kinds of cognitive skills taught in the resilience programmes surveyed in the previous chapter.

Dillen puts this in specifically Christian terms; not that God and resilience are synonyms, but '[t]he belief in God may be a stimulus to believe in the possibility and the value of resilience'.[11] This builds on previous research that shows belief in God helps resilience.[12] Dillen is wary of making religion purely functional; Christians and others do not believe in their religions simply because of the health benefits they might bring! Nonetheless, resilience 'may be seen as a life experience that gives people a glimpse of what resurrection could be like'.[13]

Reutter and Bigatti (2014) refine the concepts, distinguishing between spirituality, which is to do with daily spiritual experiences, and religiosity, which is more about adherence to a religion.[14] Both help resilience, but they are different. Religiosity involves holding religious values, belief and practices, such as public worship; spirituality is more internal, personal and subjective. One can be religious without being spiritual, and vice versa.

---

9 Gnanaprakash, 'Spirituality and resilience among post-graduate university students'.

10 Gnanaprakash, 'Spirituality and resilience among post-graduate university students', p 393.

11 A Dillen, 'The resiliency of children and spirituality: a practical theological reflection', *International Journal of Children's Spirituality*, 17.1, 2012, pp 61-75, p 67.

12 S Thwala and A Gunnestad, 'Resilience and religion in children and youth in Southern Africa', *International Journal of Children's Spirituality*, 16.2, 2011, pp 169-185.

13 A Dillen, 'The resiliency of children and spirituality', p 68.

14 K K Reutter and S M Bigatti, 'Religiosity and spirituality as resiliency resources: moderation, mediation, or moderated mediation?', *Journal for the Scientific Study of Religion*, 53.1, 2014, pp 56-72.

Reutter and Bigatti's research demonstrates that both higher spirituality, and high levels of religiosity, are associated with fewer psychological problems resulting from stress. This concurs with previous studies that suggest that religiosity helps in stress because of the social resources available, whereas spirituality helps because of causal attributions; spiritually-oriented meditation is more efficacious in reducing levels of anger, anxiety and tension than nonspiritual relaxation techniques. Also spiritual attachment helps; perceived support from divinity is associated with fewer symptoms of depression and greater self-esteem among individuals experiencing high levels of stress, and is also associated with increased optimism, hope, inner strength and self-actualisation.

Kim and Esquivel also distinguish between spirituality and religiosity, seeing religion as a system of beliefs, feelings and actions shared by a group, which provides the basis for transcendental values that guide ethical, moral and interpersonal conduct; while spirituality is a universal phenomenon, inherent to human nature and may have a biological basis. Its development is lifelong, emerging in childhood and becoming a search for purpose and longing for transcendental meaning. Religiosity involves three distinct orientations: ritual or liturgical practices (extrinsic), adopting a belief system and doctrines (intrinsic) and seeking to relate to the divine (search). Spirituality can overlap with all three but most closely parallels a search orientation.[15]

Kim and Esquival argue from the literature that religion and spirituality are protective resilience factors. Spiritual values serve to maintain an optimistic outlook on life and help one to find meaning in adverse situations. Spirituality gives close relationships, social support, moral conduct, personal growth, adaptive coping and development of meaning and purpose in life, and so resilience. Greater spiritual wellbeing is a predictor of lower anxiety. There is a high relation between religiosity and psychological wellbeing in all age groups, daily spiritual experiences being the most important part. For this reason, Kim and Esquival encourage schools, families and churches to promote the development of spirituality in adolescents.

Manning agrees that spirituality is a powerful coping mechanism; religion and spirituality provide people with a source of hope, comfort and resilience in the face of adversity.[16] For the women in her study,

---

15 S Kim and G B Esquivel, 'Adolescent spirituality and resilience: theory, research, and educational practices', *Psychology in the Schools,* 48.7, 2011, pp 755-765.

16 Manning, 'Navigating hardships in old age'.

spirituality served as a pathway to resilience. Resilience was how they experienced the functional aspect of their spirituality.

> In other words, resilience was a process with an outcome of being successful in adaptation to adversity. More specifically, spirituality was a pathway to resilience, which led to subjective well-being.[17]

Another interesting aspect of Manning's study was that the women in the study demonstrably became better at being resilient as they got older – a capacity that Manning called 'accumulated resilience'. Manning concluded that the fact that spirituality develops resilience is a causal factor in the documented positive connections between spirituality and subjective wellbeing.

It is also notable that older adults who score high on resilience scales 'story', or narrate, their lives in identifiable ways. High resilience is associated with telling one's life story as 'redemptive sequences' – how they grew from adversity, not just that it happened or that it contaminated them. Such people also communicate a sense of narrative agency – they felt they had a story to tell; and a narrative openness – the feeling life is going somewhere, and they are open to whatever comes. This correlated with a strong positivity, and a sense of things happening for a reason. All the high scorers studied also identified with a larger reality, God or some higher power, and a sense of existential security. Lower scorers on the resilience scale tended to have more negative narrative styles; they also were more questioning and less certain as regards spiritual matters.[18] This is congruent with earlier research, suggesting that spirituality and religion serve people's need to give meaning to life events.[19]

A concept related to spirituality is 'spiritual intelligence', which addresses problems of meaning and value. Khosravi and Nikmanesh demonstrate that spiritual intelligence has a positive association with resilience. This, they add, is not surprising given that other research shows components of resilience are hopefulness, personal control, coping, and religiosity/spirituality. Spiritual intelligence is more specific, including neurological processes, particular cognitive capabilities and spiritual persona and interest.

> Spiritual intelligence is concerned with the internal life of mind and spirit and its association with being in the world. It implies a

17 Manning, 'Navigating hardships in old age', p 571.

18 Randall *et al*, 'Narrative and resilience'.

19 Greene, Galambos and Lee; 'Resilience theory', p 82.

> capability for a deep understanding of existential questions and insight into multiple levels of conscious. It is more than individual mental skill. In addition to self-awareness, it implies awareness of our relationship to the transcendent, to each other, to the earth and all beings.[20]

Grafton, Gillespie and Henderson also write of spiritual intelligence – 'a sense of life meaning, purpose, or power from within or from a transcendent source such as God', which 'encompasses a way of being, learning, and finding one's place and meaningful purpose in the greater scheme of the universe'.[21] Their concern is for oncology nurses to learn resilience. They call for employers to provide ongoing cognitive education to develop emotional and spiritual intelligence, as well as techniques for relaxation. Similarly, Hesketh, Ivy and Smith advocate spirituality as developing resiliency for police; they define spirituality broadly, including things such as feeling part of a community, feeling supported, recognised, important and valued, feeling connected to others and feeling work has meaning and purpose.[22]

More specifically, forgiveness is a highly resilient response. Wade Tucker and Cornish recommend forgiveness interventions, to train and help people to forgive.[23] Other spiritual values would seem to be backed up by the neuroscience of empathy. The human brain, research suggests, is set up to share others' emotional states and to empathise. If this is transformed into concern for the wellbeing of the other, resilience is fostered. If it becomes personal distress it weakens resilience. In addition, resilient individuals could be characterised by a stronger vicarious response to others' joy.[24]

In other words, it seems that although burnout for clergy is a serious problem, the resources necessary for developing resilience and avoiding burnout are their very stock in trade. There are remarkable overlaps between aspects of resilience and traditional Christian spirituality. As well as the specific value of spirituality in resilience, almost all of the other qualities that are recommended for promoting resilience are precisely those that come out of Christian thinking.

---

20 Khosravi and Nikmanesh, 'Relationship of spiritual intelligence with resilience and perceived stress', p 52.

21 Grafton, Gillespie and Henderson, 'Resilience', p 703.

22 Hesketh, Ivy and Smith, 'Keeping the Peelian spirit'.

23 Wade, Tucker and Cornish, 'Forgiveness interventions and the promotion of resilience'.

24 Hein, 'Empathy and resilience in a connected world'.

5. How Christian spirituality overlaps with resilience research

5.1. *Adversity leads to strength*

At a very basic level, resilience research explodes the idea that the good life is the trouble-free life. Traditionally, there has been a tendency to assume that negative life circumstances impede positive adaptation. However, research suggests that people with a history of some lifetime adversity reported better mental health and well-being outcomes than people whose lives have been trouble-free. It seems that there is such a thing as 'stress inoculation'; moderate exposure to hardship helps people to use their resources, such as taking advantage of social support, and gives them a sense of hope for future trials.[1] Resilience is built in a context of stress.[2]

This can only be good news to people who not only recognise that life is inevitably difficult for anyone in a fallen world, but who are deliberately going into work which will attract opposition and difficulty. All humans born into the world cursed as a result of sin will struggle as they face relationship pain and physical hardship (Genesis 3:14-19). All Christians trying to lead a godly life in Christ Jesus will be persecuted (2 Timothy 3:12). Those who are in Christian *leadership* will have to endure suffering as people's itching ears reject the truth they do not want to hear (2 Timothy 4:3-5).

The Bible recognises, however, that whatever suffering we endure, God can use it for good. Christian teaching points to the growth that can result from suffering in life (Romans 5:3-5). What people need, it seems, is not a stress-free life, but the framework to treat stress well; to use it as a stimulus for growth, rather than buckling under it. It seems from the literature that the framework in which stress is interpreted is key for this; people need to be able to interpret the stressor as part of a larger story, rather than meaningless or random. This leads us to our next aspect of resilience.

---

1 Fletcher and Sarkar, 'Psychological resilience'.

2 Doney, 'Fostering resilience'.

5.2. *Sense of meaning and purpose*

It is clear that a sense of meaning to life – that it is not random and arbitrary – and a sense of purpose – that it is heading somewhere – are key psychological factors in creating resilience. This is central to the research that highlights spirituality and religiosity as important to resilience.

Christian doctrine holds that humans have been created by God, in his image, and are loved by him, and so are not only valuable in and of themselves but are *meaningful*. Life is not random, but given by a loving God who wants us to thrive. Moreover, we were created *for* a purpose, essentially for Christ (Colossians 1:16); which would suggest that humans have an innate orientation towards worship. This would explain the universal sense of spirituality that is commented on in so many research articles.

Moreover, it is not just humans who have been created valuable, meaningful and purposeful, but everything else as well. Christian teaching holds to a sovereign creator God who upholds and maintains the universe, taking it to its ultimate goal of renewal through Christ. Humans are part of this universal plan; their lives are not too small to be God's concerns. As such, nothing happens at random. Life events, even painful ones, are deliberate parts of God's plan. Christians can look upon suffering as something that is temporary and resulting in good, even if unpleasant at the time (1 Peter 1:4-5, Romans 8:18).

5.3. *Transcendence*

Related to a sense of meaning and purpose is the sense of transcendence that some of the resilience literature refers to. This is a sense of connectedness to something greater; the idea that we are not alone, not isolated, we have a connection to a higher reality.

Christians know this personal connection with God. Doctrinally, Jesus' death in providing forgiveness of sins allows Christians to approach God directly (Hebrews 10:19-22); as the famous hymn has it, 'Bold I approach the eternal throne'. The incarnation itself, Jesus coming to earth as a man, emphasises the reality of direct contact with God, initiated by God and graciously made possible by him. Personal relationship with God is taught and modelled Sunday by Sunday in church services; it is also lived out daily in personal prayer and Bible reading, as individuals respond to and talk directly to God. It is a daily and very real experience for Christians.

5.4. *Hope and optimism and positive emotions*

As we have seen, positive emotions are central to the traits that promote resilience.

The Christian faith is built around hope – one of the three 'things that abide' in 1 Corinthians 13:13. The future of heaven is certain because it has been promised by God, who always keeps his promises and does not change (Exodus 34:6). So no matter how bad things may get, they will always get better. I have put the quality of 'hope' together with 'optimism' here, for it seems to me they are very closely linked. The optimism that is written of as being so important to resilience refers to a generally positive view in life, an outlook that expects there to be a good outcome in the future, and finds reason for positive emotions.

This seems to be closely related to the biblical concept of 'joy'. Joy can be a difficult concept for Christians to grasp – even if they experience it – for the Bible commands joy, and what is more, commands it even in the midst of suffering. This seems odd – how can an emotion be commanded, and how can it be commanded when there is no reason to feel positive?

The biblical answer is that, for Christians, there is always reason to feel positive, even when circumstances are bad. This is precisely because of the biblical concept of hope. No matter how bad life may get now, there is always a bright future, which is certain, and which puts all current suffering into perspective (1 Peter 1:4-5, 6-7; Romans 8:18). This seems to be precisely the kind of cognitive reappraisal recommended by the resilience research. There is always a 'silver lining' (the growth that comes through suffering, the good that God will work in all things), and there is always a 'light at the end of the tunnel' (the hope of heaven) – suffering is never in itself reason to despair.

5.5. *Altruism*

The kind of outward focus and other-person awareness that characterises altruism has been frequently mentioned in the resilience literature as promotive a resilient personality. Again, this resonates strongly with Christian spirituality.

God is one who is essentially altruistic, other-person-centred (or, even more fundamentally, 'loving'). The doctrine of the Trinity emphasises this. God is not one alone; he is three in one, each person caring for the good of the other two. This altruism is also enacted in salvation history, as

God cares for humans so much that he sent his son, the second person of the Trinity, to earth to suffer and die for their sakes (John 3:16). It is also shown in the Son himself, who was willing to give up his place as God to limit himself in human form and suffer death, for the sake of others (Philippians 2:6-8). This value of love for others, then, is absolutely central to Christianity. It has been reflected in Christian history first and foremost with the spread of the saving message itself, and also with the establishment of schools, hospitals, care for the poor and charity; it is still a reality for Christians who live out what they profess.

5.6. *Self-efficacy: God efficacy*

One of the frequently emphasised qualities that promotes resilience is self-efficacy, the belief that one can accomplish one's given tasks. This seems closely linked to hope and a general positivity in life, which as seen above is part of Christian spirituality. However the resilience literature also refers to more specific beliefs and confidence in one's own powers.

Here it seems that the resilience literature parts from Christian spirituality. For although the Bible recommends people be rational and sensible in their evaluations, this includes sensible evaluation of limitations. Sometimes the resilience literature seems to be recommending quite a baseless self-confidence. After all, humans are limited; there are many things in life we cannot control.

However, I would suggest that Christian spirituality offers something better than self-efficacy, which would actually serve the purpose of resilience even more. I call this, for want of a better term, God-efficacy. Belief in a sovereign God, who wants our good, and who will accomplish his purposes, is a far stronger basis for optimism than a (possibly delusional) belief in our own powers.

5.7. *Forgiveness*

Researchers have identified forgiveness as both a trait and an activity that promotes resilience.[3]

---

3 Wade, Tucker and Cornish, 'Forgiveness interventions and the promotion of resilience'; Chesak *et al*, 'Enhancing resilience among new nurses'; Loprinzi *et al*, 'Stress management and resilience training'; A Sood *et al*, 'Stress management and resilience training among Department of Medicine faculty: a pilot randomized clinical trial', *Journal of General Internal Medicine*, 26.8, 2011, pp 858-861.

This central Christian value, forgiveness, rests on the premise that God forgives us. In the Christian view, we need forgiveness, not just for how we commonly treat each other as human beings but for how we treat God – usually as being peripheral to life, never as the wholly good creator who deserves all our love. God provides that forgiveness, making it possible by taking away all the penalty we might deserve for sin in Christ's death which paid for it all.

As a result, Christians are called upon to forgive others. It is part of the Lord's prayer. It is an inexorable logic; how can we expect God to forgive us if we are unwilling to forgive others? It is the basis of the famous parable of the unforgiving servant in Matthew 18.

It is also, as identified in resilience literature amongst a great deal of other research, an excellent social and psychological balm. Forgiveness enables individuals to let go of bitterness, which is personally poisonous in itself, and which drives spiralling cycles of social discord. Forgiveness brings relationships back together and cements social harmony. Quite apart from being commanded by God, it is an extremely useful practice. It is also terribly difficult to do, and the Christian life is ongoing practice. Mature Christians are marked by their immense capacity for forgiveness, and consequently generally show great joy; they would also, one would surmise from the literature, be able to demonstrate great resilience.

5.8. *Social network*

One of the key external factors identified in the literature as helping resilience is strong relationships, and a supportive social network.

Christianity is a very social religion. It builds communities. Christians are saved into a family, adopted as children of God (e.g. Romans 8:15, Ephesians 1:5), and become part of the body of Christ (e.g. Romans 12:5, 1 Corinthians 12:12). From the start, Christians joined together in churches, which are fundamentally for the encouragement and building up of each other (Hebrews 10:25; Ephesians 4:11-14; 1 Corinthians 12:7). It is no accident that throughout history, Christians have built communities, to live together, for study, for social care.

This building of community is the direct outflowing of other-person-centredness, to be involved with other people and to share one's life. This is linked to the virtue of hospitality and care for others

(Hebrews 13:1-3). Churches are a wonderful gift in this respect, providing an immediate social network of care.

For those in leadership, there can be some delicacy in negotiating relationships within the congregation one is working for, but whether the network is the immediate church family or wider Christian relationships, the social network is immediately there. Moreover, the social skills acquired as the daily bread-and-butter of Christian ministry can make accessing this social network much more fruitful.

5.9. *How, then, do we train Christian ministers for resilience?*

It would seem we do so by training them to be Christian. They need to be taught the content of Christianity; not just to have a slew of practical skills. Christian 'theory', it seems, even its most highfalutin theology, is very practical. Transcendence and spirituality are directly linked to the most practical of skills in coping with the dirty and stressful circumstances of life.

Christian ministers, then, need to be taught to make spirituality central to their lives. This should be a lived reality of a training college, not an optional personal extra. Staff can model and encourage this in one-to-one interaction, in tutorials, in casual encounters. It might suggest that corporate worship in chapel be frequent and compulsory, not as an institutional disciplinary tool but as a genuine aid to developing student capacities.

But overall, it is the cumulative effect of genuine deepening spirituality that would seem to be the greatest benefit a training college can give its future ministers. They need to be taught Christian doctrines about God and his purposes; about our place and value within them; about God's love and salvation and future hope. They need to make this part of a personal devotional life; that is, be taught to pray and read the Bible and meditate upon it. They need, in fact, all the traditional theological values that more recent Christian trends have tried to modernise, perhaps with quite unexpected detrimental effects on the clergy. In the midst of all the pressures to train clergy as business administrators and social workers, the basic values of their faith emerge as fundamental practical skills for their lifelong calling.

6. So what do we do? Advice for Christian ministers

6.1. Take heart: being Christian is good for you

The considerable weight of research on the human quality of resilience comes to very simple conclusions: the spiritual and moral values commanded by God are good for us. So take heart. Ministry is hard, but the very things that contribute to being the person who can deal with stress are things that should be central. Our ultimate authority is not scientific research, but the research simply confirms what we might have known from the Bible anyway. The things that are the food of Christian life – the word of God and the effects it bears within the person – are the things that, practically speaking, keep us going. It should not be surprising. We are beings created to worship God and live in obedience to him. It is not at all strange that doing this turns out to be good for us, indeed turns out to be precisely what any person needs in order to cope with the struggles and pain of ordinary life in a fallen world.

6.2. Devote yourselves to godly living

Therefore, we should reapply ourselves to personal spiritual devotions and good deeds. They were always right to do anyway, in obedience to God; now we have the added experimental evidence (not surprising, as noted above) that these things work for our good. So do them. Have a daily time with God, strengthening the lived reality of his transcendence and reapplying the truths that his purposes are real and will be worked out. Strengthen trust in God, deliberately, through bringing to mind his promises and how completely he has fulfilled them. Transform your mind by God's word. Act on his commands, in love and sacrifice for others. Forgive others as God has forgiven us. Be consciously and regularly thankful. These things do transform minds; we always knew it, now we know the brain chemistry as well.

This requires filling the mind with what is true and deliberate thinking. Just how much time do we spend in deliberate thought about God, in reflection on his goodness and how that is evident in the world, in considering others and how God would have us serve them? Just how much time do we spend on these things, in comparison with the number of hours spent absorbing and failing to notice trivial, worldly or specious teaching? Every newspaper, every billboard, every television programme, every blog or podcast or conversation or email will teach something, good or bad. How much do we deliberately ensure to be wholesome and true?

6.3. *Particular ideas for rethinking*

There may be some specific things we should rethink, biblically. The first is the role of emotions in the Christian life. Positive emotions are good for us; and positive emotions are commanded in Scripture. There is a tendency in evangelical circles to redefine emotional words (such as 'joy' and 'contentment') to evacuate their emotional content; to make them mean 'commitment' and 'lack of complaining', or similar. We can be rightly suspicious of an over-emotional, hyped or mystical Christianity which privileges feelings above rationally understood truth. In response, it can be tempting to teach that emotions are unimportant and should not be paid attention. However emotions are part of being human, and (like thoughts or actions) they can be appropriate to godly truths or not. Moreover, we should not fall into the trap of thinking that emotions are entirely fickle and beyond our control. That is not biblical, and the literature on resilience – not to mention the considerable success of techniques such as mindfulness and cognitive therapy – demonstrates it is not true.

There is a place for teaching on godly emotions, to help people develop this part of their created being towards conformity with Christ, just as they work for Christlikeness in other areas of their lives.

Similarly, we may need to rethink how we approach stress and difficulty. It is not something that can be avoided in a fallen world; and while suffering is not something we should deliberately seek, neither should we be afraid of it. If the resilience literature teaches us anything, it is the power of reframing expectations and reactions; the power of changing how we think about pain. Again, biblically this is something we always knew, although it is so very easy to forget, particularly in a world that idolises comfort. Suffering and stress, however, are normal. Moreover, they are part of God's way of developing character. It may be that it is necessary for us to be grieved by various trials, but the result will be strengthening (1 Peter 1:6-7). Suffering produces endurance, character and hope (Romans 5:3-4). We should neither expect a comfortable life, nor be thrown by difficulty. It is normal, and can result in incomparable good.

6.4. *Be aware*

Part of this reframing thought is to be more aware of oneself. This is not the same as being self-absorbed; rather, it is to think of oneself realistically. Be aware of how you react to situations. Be aware of your automatic responses, because only in being aware of them can you change them to be more godly. Understand how you tend to interpret stress, so you can deliberately challenge your assumptions to make them more God-based. Be aware of what your heart really wants to believe so you can pray about that specifically. Know where you need to challenge yourself with Scripture.

6.5. *Selecting candidates for ministry training*

To the extent that some people seem to have a better chance of resilience than others, having certain inherited or innate personal characteristics such as a naturally optimistic temperament and finding social relationships easy, then it seems these should be identified at the selection stage. It may well be useful to investigate as to whether a candidate has qualities such as a decent spiritual intelligence, low neuroticism, and prevalence of positive emotions (or clear understanding of strategies to overcome the effects of negative ones). Some people are more gifted for Christian ministry than others, as has been recognised throughout the history of the church, and it may be that characteristics that better enable one to cope with stress are part of this gifting. If there are biological or personality factors, then that just helps us identify who should and should not go into ministry. But experienced ministers are still the best judges; we should beware an overly facile adoption of literature in a developing field.

6.6. *Don't be neurotic, as individuals or groups*

We have mentioned above that people can be neurotic; expecting failure, predicting hardship, and living in fear. As we have seen, even individuals for whom this comes naturally can learn to change, and so actually work to bring about more positive outcomes. As Christians, we have every reason to challenge any kind of inbuilt neuroticism; it may be a fallen world, but we know the sovereign Lord who controls it and works in all things for the good of those who trust him.

Let us not be neurotic, then, in ourselves or in our organisations. The situation can look bleak as embattled Christians face falling numbers, a society seemingly ever more hostile to God's word and challenges from within as well as outside the church. Like Elijah, it is all too easy to assume that we, our small group – whatever it is – is all alone against overwhelming odds. As Elijah learned, that is not true; indeed, it is never true. God will work out his purposes. *That* is true. That is the basis of a true optimism, true positive emotions, true resilience that is based in reality, not wishful thinking. That is our hope.

6.7. *In conclusion*

We can be encouraged that a lot of what is recommended for building resilience for stressful lives and work places is already part of what most Christians will do daily anyway. The challenge is to do them more.

Overall, it is the cumulative effect of genuine deepening spirituality that would seem to be the best way to be prepared for stress, in a way that will enable one to come back from it even stronger. Those going into ministry need to be taught Christian doctrines about God and his purposes; about our place and value within them; about God's love and salvation and future hope. They need to be taught to pray and read the Bible and meditate upon it. In other words, they need traditional Bible-based theology. What is more, they need to be confident that it is true. The loss of biblical authority may be one of the most significant factors in the sad emotional plight of clergy across mainstream churches today. Confident pastors will negotiate suffering, opposition and emotional hardship through a life based on the thoughts, actions and motivations that come from knowing Christ through his revealed word. As the apostle puts it:

> And it is my prayer that your love may abound more and more, with knowledge and all discernment, so that you may approve what is excellent, and so be pure and blameless for the day of Christ, filled with the fruit of righteousness that comes through Jesus Christ, to the glory and praise of God (Philippians 1:9-11).

7. Appendix

7.1. *A Counselling Programme for Resilience*

As we have seen from the literature, there are a number of overlapping qualities and skills that have been experimentally verified to encourage resilience in people. While some aspects of resilience are fixed and inherited, research has also revealed that resilience can be learned. The literature includes details of a number of programmes specifically designed to produce resilience in people facing stressful occupations, including teaching, nursing, and the military. These programmes are useful, for here we see the research literature – which, as demonstrated, is immense and can be diffuse and difficult to categorise – boiled down into specific training pathways. Experts in resilience have identified the key skills that need to be taught, and traits that need to be fostered, in order to develop resilience in their clients.

Moreover, there is good experimental data demonstrating that training programmes in resilience work. They differ in teaching strategies: programmes used positive psychology techniques, Cognitive-Behavioural Therapy (CBT), transformational coping, acceptance and commitment therapy, mindfulness, interpersonal therapy, attention and interpretation therapy, and diaphragmatic breathing. Nonetheless, the overall aim of developing the key characteristics of resilience has demonstrably been met.[1]

It is informative to look at the details of a counselling programme to see an example of how a person struggling to cope can be helped to develop resilience.

7.2. *Strengths-based Cognitive-Behavioural Therapy*

Cognitive psychologists Christine Padesky and Kathleen Mooney developed a four-step model in 2001 to be carried out in one-to-one therapy with clients, in order to help them develop resilience.[2] Padesky

---

1 T Macedo *et al*, 'Building resilience for future adversity: a systematic review of interventions in non-clinical samples of adults', *BMC Psychiatry*, 14, 2014, pp 227-234.

2 C A Padesky and K A Mooney, 'Strengths-based cognitive-behavioural therapy: a four-step model to build resilience', *Clinical Psychology and Psychotherapy*, 19.4, 2012, pp 283-290.

and Mooney are amongst those who consider resilience a process, not a trait – 'the ability to cope and adapt in the face of adversity and/or to bounce back and restore positive functioning when stressors become overwhelming'.[3] This kind of resilience, Padesky and Mooney are adamant from their clinical experience, can be taught, practiced, and learned. Cited 54 times since its publication in 2012 (according to Google Scholar), their model is designed for use in therapy with clients who struggle with life in various ways and are seeking help to improve, but the principles could be applicable to mentally healthy people who face particularly high levels of stress.

The four steps of this model are:

1. Search for strengths
2. Construct a personal model of resilience (PMR)
3. Apply the PMR to areas of life difficulty and
4. Practise resilience

First, clients are asked to identify with the help of the therapist, strengths that they already have. Strengths are strategies, beliefs and personal assets used with relative ease that can promote resilience. Seven areas of competence that are empirically correlated with resilience are:

1. Good health and an easy temperament
2. Secure attachment and basic trust in other people
3. Interpersonal competence including the ability to recruit help
4. Cognitive competence that encompasses the ability to read, capacity to plan, self-efficacy and intelligence
5. Emotional competence such as the ability to regulate one's emotions, delay gratification, maintain realistically high self-esteem and employ creativity and humour to one's benefit
6. The ability and opportunity to contribute to others
7. Holding faith that your life matters and life has meaning, including a moral sense of connection to others.

---

3 Padesky and Mooney, 'Strengths-based cognitive-behavioural therapy: a four-step model to build resilience', p 283.

There are many pathways and different combinations of strengths that can lead to resilience. Therapists help clients identify the strengths they already possess and build from them.

> For example, some people have good problem solving skills combined with a flexible sense of humour and these strengths may be the basis for their resilience. Yet, another pathway to resilience could be the social ability to enlist the help of others and a belief that life's challenges have a higher purpose.[4]

The first step, then, involves identifying the person's strengths by examining something they do every day – which by definition must show resilience because everyone's days will include obstacles of one sort or another. Areas to explore include hobbies, special skill activities (music, sports, photography), caretaking activities (for pets, family or friends) or daily activities in which the person experiences proficiency and/or enjoyment (cooking, gardening, woodworking, sewing, dressing fashionably, living within a budget). Once the therapist and client choose an area of focus, they then identify strengths the client regularly exhibits in overcoming difficulties in this area.

The second step of the model involves turning this list of strengths into slightly more general resilience strategies. The example given was of a client who successfully made entries to his video blog daily. If something went wrong in the filming, he would encourage himself to keep going by remembering the people whom he knew watched his vlog daily and depended upon it. This strength could be generalised to principles such as: think about how I can help others, actively imagine other people and how I am helping them. Other potential strategies that people might invoke are: 'trust in my ability to work hard', or 'use humour'.

Then the therapist and client would consider how these strategies might help in problem areas. 'The focus of these discussions is on staying resilient in the face of difficulties rather than success in solving or overcoming them.'[5] So, for instance, a client reported having difficulties when his supervisor criticised him (the client thought unfairly) for poor work. The therapeutic goal was not (necessarily) to stop the supervisor from being critical, but for the client to stay positive despite the criticism, by using his strategies. The client suggested that

---

4 Padesky and Mooney, 'Strengths-based cognitive-behavioural therapy: a four-step model to build resilience', p 285.

5 Padesky and Mooney, 'Strengths-based cognitive-behavioural therapy: a four-step model to build resilience', p 287.

when the supervisor was critical, the client could tell himself: 'He usually only criticizes one person per shift. I can stand up and be the one to take it for my work group'.[6] In other words, altruistic thinking would give him the strength to handle the criticism.

Finally, the client puts the strategy into practice, as is typical with Cognitive-Behavioural Therapy. The client and the therapist plan a specific experiment, write down beforehand what might happen (predictions about the client's resilience), and expected thoughts and feelings. Afterwards, the client evaluates the outcome in terms of resilience rather than any other outcome (for example, the evaluation criterion might be 'did I stay calm while my supervisor was criticising me' rather than 'did he praise me instead of criticising'). Some clients report this is win-win; if there is a good outcome, they win; if the outcome is poor, they still win by getting to practise resilience.

Throughout the paper, Padesky and Mooney also emphasise how the attitude of the therapist helps the client develop resilience skills; simply an increased use of smiling helps. Use of imagery and metaphors, thought up by the client, are very helpful. In other words, engaging the client's emotions positively is a clear part of the development of psychological resilience in the face of difficulty.

---

6 Padesky and Mooney, 'Strengths-based cognitive-behavioural therapy: a four-step model to build resilience', p 287.

8. Bibliography

Allain-Chapman, J. 2012, *Resilient Pastors: The Role of Adversity in Healing and Growth* (London: SPCK).

Alvord, M. K. and Grados, J. J. 2005, 'Enhancing Resilience in Children: A Proactive Approach', *Professional Psychology: Research and Practice,* vol. 36, no. 3, pp 238-245.

American Psychological Association, 2016. 'The Road to Resilience: What is resilience?' http://www.apa.org/helpcenter/road-resilience.aspx.

Aranda, K. and Hart, A. 2015, 'Resilient moves: Tinkering with practice theory to generate new ways of thinking about using resilience', *Health,* vol. 19, no. 4, pp 355-371.

Arnetz, B. B., Nevedal, D. C., Lumley, M. A., Backman, L. and Lublin, A. 2009, 'Trauma resilience training for police: Psychophysiological and performance effects', *Journal of Police and Criminal Psychology,* vol. 24, no. 1, pp 1-9.

Arthur, J., Hedges, L. V., Coe, R. and Waring, M. 2012, *Research Methods and Methodologies in Education* (Los Angeles: Sage).

Atkinson, P. A., Martin, C. R. and Rankin, J. 2009, 'Resilience revisited', *Journal of psychiatric and mental health nursing,* vol. 16, no. 2, pp 137-145.

Bardoel, E. A., Pettit, T. M., De Cieri, H. and McMillan, L. 2014, 'Employee resilience: an emerging challenge for HRM', *Asia Pacific Journal of Human Resources,* vol. 52, no. 3, pp 279-297.

Beebe, R. S. 2007, 'Predicting Burnout, Conflict Management Style, and Turnover Among Clergy', *Journal of Career Assessment,* vol. 15, no. 2, pp 257-275.

Bianchi, R., Schonfeld, I. S. and Laurent, E. 2015, 'Burnout–depression overlap: a review', *Clinical Psychology Review,* vol. 36, pp 28-41.

Block, J. H. and Block, J. 1980, 'The role of ego-control and ego-resiliency in the organization of behavior', in *Development of Cognition, Affect, and Social Relations: The Minnesota Symposia on Child Psychology,* ed. W. Andrew Collins, Vol. 13, (New York and London: Psychology Press) pp 39-69.

Boden, M. T., Kulkarni, M., Shurick, A., Bonn-Miller, M. O. and Gross, J. 2014, 'Responding to Trauma and Loss' in *The Resilience Handbook: Approaches to Stress and Trauma,* eds. M. Kent, M. C. Davis and J. W. Reich (New York and London: Routledge) pp 86-99.

Bonanno, G. A., Westphal, M. and Mancini, A. D. 2012, 'Loss, Trauma, and Resilience in adulthood', *Annual Review of Gerontology and Geriatrics,* vol. 32, no. 1, pp 189-210.

Bonanno, G. A. 2012, 'Uses and abuses of the resilience construct: Loss, trauma, and health-related adversities', *Social Science and Medicine,* vol. 74, no. 5, pp 753-756.

Bottrell, D. 2009, 'Understanding 'marginal' perspectives: towards a social theory of resilience', *Qualitative Social Work,* vol. 8, no. 3, pp 321-339.

Bouillet, D., Pavin Ivanec, T. and Miljević-Riđički, R. 2014, 'Preschool teachers' resilience and their readiness for building children's resilience', *Health Education,* vol. 114, no. 6, pp 435-450.

Bryman, A. 2012, *Social Research Method,* 4th edn, Oxford University Press, Oxford.

Burns, Bob and Chapman, Tasha D. 2013, *Resilient Ministry: What Pastors Told Us About Surviving and Thriving* (Downers Grove, IL: IVP).

Burns, Jay, 2015, *Resilience: A Biblical, Gospel-centred Guide to Long-Term Fruitfulness and Joy in the Service of Jesus Christ* (Kindle Edition).

Chaskalson, Michael, 2014, *Mindfulness in Eight Weeks* (London: HarperThorsons).

Chesak, S. S., Bhagra, A., Schroeder, D. R., Foy, D. A., Cutshall, S. M. and Sood, A. 2015, 'Enhancing resilience among new nurses: feasibility and efficacy of a pilot intervention', *The Ochsner Journal,* vol. 15, no. 1, pp 38-44.

Cohn, M. A., Fredrickson, B. L., Brown, S. L., Mikels, J. A. and Conway, A. M. 2009, 'Happiness unpacked: positive emotions increase life satisfaction by building resilience', *Emotion,* vol. 9, no. 3, pp 361-368.

Connor, K. M. and Davidson, J. R. 2003, 'Development of a new resilience scale: The Connor-Davidson resilience scale (CD-RISC)', *Depression and Anxiety,* vol. 18, no. 2, pp 76-82.

Cornum, R., Matthews, M. D. and Seligman, M. E. 2011, 'Comprehensive soldier fitness: building resilience in a challenging institutional context', *American Psychologist,* vol. 66, no. 1, pp 4-9.

Davis, J. S. 2013, 'Building resilient students: three strategies for success', *Educational Horizons,* vol. 92, no. 2, pp 21-25.

Dillen, A. 2012, 'The resiliency of children and spirituality: a practical theological reflection', *International Journal of Children's Spirituality,* vol. 17, no. 1, pp 61-75.

Doney, P.A. 2013, 'Fostering resilience: a necessary skill for teacher retention', *Journal of Science Teacher Education,* vol. 24, no. 4, pp 645-664.

Dwiwardani, C., Hill, P. C., Bollinger, R. A., Marks, L. E., Steele, J. R., Doolin, H. N., Wood, S. L., Hook, J. N. and Davis, D. E. 2014, 'Virtues develop from a secure base: attachment and resilience as predictors of humility, gratitude, and forgiveness', *Journal of Psychology and Theology,* vol. 42, no. 1, pp 83-90.

Easterbrooks, M. A., Ginsburg, K. and Lerner, R. M. 2013, 'Resilience among Military Youth', *The Future of Children,* vol. 23, no. 2, pp 99-120.

Ebersöhn, L. 2014, 'Teacher resilience: theorizing resilience and poverty', *Teachers and Teaching,* vol. 20, no. 5, pp 568-594.

Edwards, A. and Griffiths, A. 2014, 'Special issue: teachers and resilience: interdisciplinary accounts', *Teachers and Teaching,* vol. 20, no. 5, pp 499-501.

Eisold, B. K. 2005, 'Notes on lifelong resilience: perceptual and personality factors implicit in the creation of a particular adaptive style', *Psychoanalytic Psychology*, vol. 22, no. 3, pp 411-425.

Evers, W. and Tomic, W. 2003, 'Burnout among Dutch Reformed Pastors', *Journal of Psychology and Theology*, vol. 31, no. 4, pp 329-338.

Fava, G.A. and Tomba, E. 2009, 'Increasing psychological well-being and resilience by psychotherapeutic methods', *Journal of Personality*, vol. 77, no. 6, pp 1903-1934.

Feder, A., Nestler, E. J., Westphal, M. and Charney, D. S. 2010, 'Psychobiological mechanisms of resilience to stress' in *Handbook of Adult Resilience*, eds. J. W. Reich, A. J. Zautra and J. S. Hall (New York: Guilford Press) pp 35-54.

Fletcher, D. and Sarkar, M. 2013, 'Psychological resilience: a review and critique of definitions, concepts, and theory', *European Psychologist*, vol. 18, no. 1, pp 12-23.

Frijling, J. L., van Zuiden, M., Koch, S. B., Nawijn, L., Veltman, D. and Olff, M. 2014, 'Promoting Resilience After Trauma' in *The Resilience Handbook: Approaches to Stress and Trauma*, eds. M. Kent, M. C. Davis and J. W. Reich (New York and London: Routledge) pp 299-308.

Fuller M. and Fleming, K. 2005. 'Bridging a gap: a curriculum uniting competencies and theological disciplines', *Journal of Adult Theological Education* vol. 2, no. 2, pp 163-178.

Gallacher, J., Mitchell, C., Heslop, L. and Christopher, G. 2012, 'Resilience to health related adversity in older people', *Quality in Ageing and Older Adults*, vol. 13, no. 3, pp 197-204.

Garmezy, N.E. and Rutter, M.E. 1983, 'Stress, coping, and development in children.', *Seminar on Stress and Coping in Children, 1979, Ctr for Advanced Study in the Behavioral Sciences*, Johns Hopkins University Press, Stanford, CA.

Gartrell, D. and Cairone, K. B. 2014, 'Fostering resilience: teaching social-emotional skills', *YC Young Children*, vol. 69, no. 3, pp 92-93.

Gillespie, B. M., Chaboyer, W., Wallis, M. and Grimbeek, P. 2007, 'Resilience in the operating room: developing and testing of a resilience model', *Journal of Advanced Nursing*, vol. 59, no. 4, pp 427-438.

Gnanaprakash, C. 2013, 'Spirituality and resilience among post-graduate university students', *Journal of Health Management*, vol. 15, no. 3, pp 383-396.

Golden, J., Piedmmont, R. L., Clarrocchi, J. W. and Rodgerson, T. 2004, 'Spirituality and burnout: an incremental validity study', *Journal of Psychology and Theology*, vol. 32, no. 2, pp 115-125.

Grafton, E., Gillespie, B. and Henderson, S. 2010, 'Resilience: the power within', *Oncology Nursing Forum*, vol. 37, no. 6, pp 698-705.

Greene, R., Galambos, C. and Lee, Y. 2004; 2003, 'Resilience theory: theoretical and professional conceptualizations', *Journal of Human Behavior in the Social Environment*, vol. 8, no. 4, pp 75-91.

Griffiths, A. 2014, 'Promoting resilience in schools: a view from occupational health psychology', *Teachers and Teaching*, vol. 20, no. 5, pp 655-666.

Hall, P. Cougar and West, J. H. 2012, 'Boundin': responding to life challenges with resilience', *Journal of School Health*, vol. 82, no. 4, pp 196-200.

Hein, G. 2014, 'Empathy and resilience in a connected world' in *The Resilience Handbook: Approaches to Stress and Trauma*, eds. M. Kent, M. C. Davis and J. W. Reich (New York and London: Routledge) pp 144-155.

Hesketh, I., Ivy, J. and Smith, J. 2014, 'Keeping the Peelian spirit: resilience and spirituality in policing', *The Police Journal: Theory, Practice and Principles*, vol. 87, no. 3, pp 154-166.

Heywood, D. 2013. 'Educating ministers of character: building character into the learning process in ministerial formation', *Journal of Adult Theological Education*, vol. 10, no. 1, pp 4-24.

Higton, M. 2006, *Vulnerable Learning: Thinking Theologically about Higher Education*, Cambridge: Grove Books.

Hodges, D.A. 2014, 'Music as an agent of resilience' in *The Resilience Handbook: Approaches to Stress and Trauma*, eds. M. Kent, M. C. Davis and J. W. Reich (New York and London: Routledge, 2014) pp 100-112.

Hodges, H. F., Keeley, A. C. and Grier, E. C. 2005, 'Professional resilience, practice longevity, and Parse's theory for baccalaureate education', *The Journal of Nursing Education*, vol. 44, no. 12, pp 548-554.

Hong, J. Y. 2012, 'Why do some beginning teachers leave the school, and others stay? Understanding teacher resilience through psychological lenses', *Teachers and Teaching*, vol. 18, no. 4, pp 417-440.

Hu, T., Zhang, D. and Wang, J. 2015, 'A meta-analysis of the trait resilience and mental health', *Personality and Individual Differences*, vol. 76, pp 18-27.

Iacoviello, B. M. and Charney, D. S. 2014, 'Psychosocial facets of resilience: implications for preventing posttrauma psychopathology, treating trauma survivors, and enhancing community resilience', *European Journal of Psychotraumatology*, vol. 5, pp 1-10.

Johnson, D. C., Thom, N. J., Stanley, E. A., Haase, L., Simmons, A. N., Shih, P. B., Thompson, W. K., Potterat, E. G., Minor, T. R. and Paulus, M. P. 2014, 'Modifying resilience mechanisms in at-risk individuals: a controlled study of mindfulness training in Marines preparing for deployment', *The American Journal of Psychiatry*, vol. 171, no. 8, pp 844-853.

Kent, M., Davis, M. C. and Reich, J. W. 2014, *The Resilience Handbook: Approaches to Stress and Trauma* (New York and London: Routledge).

Khosravi, M. and Nikmanesh, Z. 2014, 'Relationship of spiritual intelligence with resilience and perceived stress', *Iranian Journal of Psychiatry and Behavioral Sciences*, vol. 8, no. 4, pp 52-56.

Kim, J. W., Lee, H. and Lee, K. 2013, 'Influence of temperament and character on resilience', *Comprehensive Psychiatry*, vol. 54, no. 7, pp 1105-1110.

Kim, S. and Esquivel, G. B. 2011, 'Adolescent spirituality and resilience: Theory, research, and educational practices', *Psychology in the Schools*, vol. 48, no. 7, pp 755-765.

Lankford, V. 2012, 'My whole life is plan B: a psychological and practical approach to resilience', *Transactional Analysis Journal*, vol. 42, no. 1, pp 62-70.

Le Cornu, R., Hunter, J., Down, B., Sullivan, A., Johnson, B., Peters, J. and Pearce, J. 2014, 'Promoting early career teacher resilience: a framework for understanding and acting', *Teachers and Teaching*, vol. 20, no. 5, pp 530-546.

Lee, J. H., Nam, S. K., Kim, A., Kim, B., Lee, M. Y. and Lee, S. M. 2013, 'Resilience: a meta-analytic approach', *Journal of Counseling and Development*, vol. 91, no. 3, pp 269-279.

Lemery-Chalfant, K. 2010, 'Genes and environments: How they work together to promote resilience' in *Handbook of Adult Resilience*, eds. J. W. Reich, A. J. Zautra and J. S. Hall (New York: Guilford Press, 2010) pp 55-80.

Leppin, A. L., Gionfriddo, M. R., Sood, A., Montori, V. M., Erwin, P. J., Zeballos-Palacios, C., Bora, P. R., Dulohery, M. M., Brito, J. P., Boehmer, K. R. and Tilburt, J. C. 2014, 'The efficacy of resilience training programs: a systematic review protocol', *Systematic Reviews*, vol. 3, no. 1, pp 1-5.

Lightsey, O. R. 2006, 'Resilience, meaning, and well-being', *The Counseling Psychologist*, vol. 34, no. 1, pp 96-107.

Loprinzi, C. E., Prasad, K., Schroeder, D. R. and Sood, A. 2011, 'Stress Management and Resilience Training (SMART) program to decrease stress and enhance resilience among breast cancer survivors: a pilot randomized clinical trial', *Clinical Breast Cancer*, vol. 11, no. 6, pp 364-368.

Lü, W., Wang, Z., Liu, Y. and Zhang, H. 2014, 'Resilience as a mediator between extraversion, neuroticism and happiness, PA and NA', *Personality and Individual Differences*, vol. 63, pp 128-133.

Lyons, S. T., Schweitzer, L. and Ng, E. S. W. 2015, 'Resilience in the modern career', *Career Development International*, vol. 20, no. 4, pp 363-383.

Macedo, T., Wilheim, L., Gonçalves, R., Coutinho, E. S. F., Vilete, L., Figueira, I. and Ventura, P. 2014, 'Building resilience for future adversity: a systematic review of interventions in non-clinical samples of adults', *BMC Psychiatry*, vol. 14, pp 227-234.

Manning, L. K. 2013, 'Navigating hardships in old age: exploring the relationship between spirituality and resilience in later life', *Qualitative Health Research*, vol. 23, no. 4, pp 568-575.

Mansfield, C., Beltman, S. and Price, A. 2014, ''I'm coming back again!' The resilience process of early career teachers', *Teachers and Teaching*, vol. 20, no. 5, pp 547-567.

Masten, A. S. 2001, 'Ordinary magic: resilience processes in development', *American Psychologist*, vol. 56, no. 3, pp 227-238.

Mayer, J. D. and Faber, M. A. 2010, 'Personal intelligence and resilience' in *Handbook of Adult Resilience*, eds. J. W. Reich, A. J. Zautra and J. S. Hall, (New York: Guilford Press) pp 94-111.

Miller, A. and Gibbs, S. 2014, 'Teachers' resilience and well-being: a role for educational psychology', *Teachers and Teaching*, vol. 20, no. 5, pp 609-621.

Miner, M. H., Dowson, M. and Sterland, S. 2010, 'Ministry orientation and ministry outcomes: evaluation of a new multidimensional model of clergy burnout and job satisfaction', *Journal of Occupational and Organizational Psychology*, vol. 83, no. 1, pp 167-188.

Miner, M., Sterland, S. and Dowson, M. 2009, 'Orientation to the demands of ministry: construct validity and relationship with burnout', *Review of Religious Research*, vol. 50, no. 4, pp 463-479.

Monzani, D., Steca, P., Greco, A., D'Addario, M., Pancani, L. and Cappelletti, E. 2015, 'Effective pursuit of personal goals: The fostering effect of dispositional optimism on goal commitment and goal progress', *Personality and Individual Differences*, vol. 82, pp 203-214.

Morrison, G. and Allen, M. 2007, 'Promoting student resilience in school contexts', *Theory Into Practice*, vol. 46, no. 2, pp 162-169.

Ong, A. D., Bergeman, C. and Chow, S. 2010, 'Positive emotions as a basic building block of resilience in adulthood', in *Handbook of Adult Resilience*, eds. J. W. Reich, A. J. Zautra and J. S. Hall, (New York: Guilford Press) pp 81-93.

Padesky, C. A. and Mooney, K. A. 2012, 'Strengths-based cognitive-behavioural therapy: a four-step model to build resilience', *Clinical Psychology and Psychotherapy*, vol. 19, no. 4, pp 283-290.

Panksepp, J. 2014, 'Seeking and loss in the ancestral genesis of resilience, depression, and addiction' in *The Resilience Handbook: Approaches to Stress and Trauma*, eds. M. Kent, M. C. Davis and J. W. Reich (New York and London: Routledge) pp 1-14.

Papatraianou, L. H., Levine, D. and West, D. 2014, 'Resilience in the face of cyberbullying: an ecological perspective on young people's experiences of online adversity', *Pastoral Care in Education*, vol. 32, no. 4, pp 264-283.

Park, C., Slattery, J., Kent, M., Davis, M. and Reich, J. 2014, 'Resilience interventions with a focus on meaning and values' in *The Resilience Handbook: Approaches to Stress and Trauma*, eds. M. Kent, M. C. Davis and J. W. Reich (New York and London: Routledge) pp 270-282.

Peters, J. and Pearce, J. 2012, 'Relationships and early career teacher resilience: a role for school principals', *Teachers and Teaching*, vol. 18, no. 2, pp 249-262.

Pidgeon, A. M., Ford, L. and Klaassen, F. 2014, 'Evaluating the effectiveness of enhancing resilience in human service professionals using a retreat-based Mindfulness with Metta Training Program: a randomised control trial', *Psychology, Health and Medicine*, vol. 19, no. 3, pp 355-364.

Raglan, G. B. and Schulkin, J. 2014, 'Introduction to allostasis and allostatic load' in *The Resilience Handboook: Approaches to Stress and Trauma*, eds. M. Kent, M. C. Davis and J. W. Reich (New York and London: Routledge) pp 44-52.

Randall, K. J. 2004, 'Burnout as a predictor of leaving Anglican parish ministry', *Review of Religious Research*, vol. 46, no. 1, pp 20-26.

Randall, W., Baldwin, C., McKenzie-Mohr, S., McKim, E. and Furlong, D. 2015, 'Narrative and resilience: A comparative analysis of how older adults story their lives', *Journal of Aging Studies*, vol. 34, pp 155-161.

Reich, J. W., Zautra, A. J. and Hall, J. S. 2010, *Handbook of Adult Resilience* (New York: Guilford Press).

Reivich, K. J., Seligman, M. E. and McBride, S. 2011, 'Master resilience training in the US Army', *American Psychologist*, vol. 66, no. 1, pp 25-34.

Reutter, K. K. and Bigatti, S. M. 2014, 'Religiosity and spirituality as resiliency resources: moderation, mediation, or moderated mediation?', *Journal for the Scientific Study of Religion*, vol. 53, no. 1, pp 56-72.

Richardson, G. E. 2002, 'The metatheory of resilience and resiliency', *Journal of Clinical Psychology*, vol. 58, no. 3, pp 307-321.

Robinson, J. S., Larson, C. L. and Cahill, S. P. 2014, 'Relations between resilience, positive and negative emotionality, and symptoms of anxiety and depression', *Psychological Trauma: Theory, Research, Practice, and Policy*, vol. 6, Suppl 1, pp S92-S98.

Rutter, M. 1985, 'Resilience in the face of adversity. Protective factors and resistance to psychiatric disorder', *The British Journal of Psychiatry: The Journal of Mental Science*, vol. 147, pp 598-611.

- 1987, 'Psychosocial resilience and protective mechanisms', *American Journal of Orthopsychiatry*, vol. 57, no. 3, pp 316-331.

- 2012, 'Resilience as a dynamic concept', *Development and Psychopathology*, vol. 24, no. 2, pp 335-344.

Rutter, M. L., Kreppner, J. M., O'Connor, T. G. and English and Romanian Adoptees (ERA) study team 2001, 'Specificity and heterogeneity in children's responses to profound institutional privation', *The British Journal of Psychiatry: The Journal of Mental Science*, vol. 179, pp 97-103.

Sarubin, N., Wolf, M., Giegling, I., Hilbert, S., Naumann, F., Gutt, D., Jobst, A., Sabaß, L., Falkai, P., Rujescu, D., Bühner, M. and Padberg, F. 2015, 'Neuroticism and extraversion as mediators between positive/negative life events and resilience', *Personality and Individual Differences*, vol. 82, pp 193-198.

Schwager, S. and Rothermund, K. 2014, 'The automatic basis of resilience' in *The Resilience Handbook: Approaches to Stress and Trauma*, eds. M. Kent, M. C. Davis and J. W. Reich (New York and London: Routledge) pp 55-72.

Searby, Mark A. 2015, *The Resilient Pastor: Ten Principles for Developing Pastoral Resilience* (Eugene, Oregon: Resource Publications).

Seligman, M. E. 1997, 'The optimistic child: a proven program to safeguard children against depression and build lifelong resilience', *Adolescence*, vol. 32, no. 126, p 502.

Seok, J., Lee, K., Kim, W., Lee, S., Kang, E., Ham, B., Yang, J. and Chae, J. 2012, 'Impact of early-life stress and resilience on patients with major depressive disorder', *Yonsei Medical Journal*, vol. 53, no. 6, pp 1093-1098.

Simeon, D., Yehuda, R., Cunill, R., Knutelska, M., Putnam, F. W. and Smith, L. M. 2007, 'Factors associated with resilience in healthy adults', *Psychoneuroendocrinology*, vol. 32, no. 8, pp 1149-1152.

Skodol, A.E. 2010, 'The resilient personality' in *Handbook of Adult Resilience*, eds. J. W. Reich, A. J. Zautra and J. S. Hall (New York: Guilford Press) pp 112-125.

Sood, A., Prasad, K., Schroeder, D. and Varkey, P. 2011, 'Stress management and resilience training among Department of Medicine faculty: a pilot randomized clinical trial', *Journal of General Internal Medicine*, vol. 26, no. 8, pp 858-861.

Swider, B. W. and Zimmerman, R. D. 2010, 'Born to burnout: A meta-analytic path model of personality, job burnout, and work outcomes', *Journal of Vocational Behavior*, vol. 76, no. 3, pp 487-506.

Tempski, P., Martins, M. A. and Paro, H. B. M. S. 2012, 'Teaching and learning resilience: a new agenda in medical education', *Medical Education*, vol. 46, no. 4, pp 345-346.

Tenhula, W. N., Nezu, A. M., Nezu, C. M., Stewart, M. O., Miller, S. A., Steele, J. and Karlin, B. E. 2014, 'Moving forward: A problem-solving training program to foster veteran resilience', *Professional Psychology: Research and Practice*, vol. 45, no. 6, pp 416-424.

Thomas, K. H. and Taylor, S. P. 2015, 'Beyond trauma treatment: mindfulness instruction in the training environment to prevent depression, lower suicide rates and improve resilience in the military and veteran communities', *Journal of Traumatic Stress Disorders and Treatment*, vol. 4, no. 2, pp np. Doi: http://dx.doi.org/10.4172/2324-8947.1000141.

Thwala, S. and Gunnestad, A. 2011, 'Resilience and religion in children and youth in Southern Africa', *International Journal of Children's Spirituality*, vol. 16, no. 2, pp 169-185.

Titus, C. S. 2006, *Resilience and the Virtue of Fortitude: Aquinas in Dialogue with the Psychosocial Sciences* (Washington DC: The Catholic University of America Press).

Tops, M., Buisman-Pijlman, F. T. and Carter, C. S. 2014, 'Oxytocin and attachment facilitate a shift from seeking novelty to recognizing and preferring familiarity' in *The Resilience Handbook: Approaches to Stress and Trauma*, eds. M. Kent, M. C. Davis and J. W. Reich (New York and London: Routledge) pp 115-130.

Tops, M., Luu, P., Boksem, M. A., Tucker, D. M., Kent, M., Davis, M. and Reich, J. 2014, 'The roles of predictive and reactive biobehavioral programs in resilience' in *The Resilience Handbook: Approaches to Stress and Trauma*, eds. M. Kent, M. C. Davis and J. W. Reich (New York and London: Routledge) pp 15-32.

Tusaie, K. and Dyer, J. 2004, 'Resilience: a historical review of the construct', *Holistic Nursing Practice*, vol. 18, no. 1, pp 3-10.

Ungar, M. 2008, 'Resilience across cultures', *British Journal of Social Work*, vol. 38, no. 2, pp 218-235.

Van Vliet, K. J. V. 2008, 'Shame and resilience in adulthood: a grounded theory study', *Journal of Counseling Psychology*, vol. 55, no. 2, pp 233-245.

Wade, N. G., Tucker, J. R. and Cornish, M. A. 2014, 'Forgiveness interventions and the promotion of resilience following interpersonal stress and trauma' in *The Resilience Handbook: Approaches to Stress and Trauma*, eds. M. Kent, M. C. Davis and J. W. Reich (New York and London: Routledge) pp 256-269.

Wagnild, G. M. and Collins, J. A. 2009, 'Assessing resilience', *Journal of Psychosocial Nursing and Mental Health Services*, vol. 47, no. 12, pp 28-33.

Walters, L., Laurence, C. O., Dollard, J., Elliott, T. and Eley, D. S. 2015, 'Exploring resilience in rural GP registrars – implications for training', *BMC Medical Education*, vol. 15, pp 110-118.

Waugh, C. E. 2014, 'The regulatory power of positive emotions in stress' in *The Resilience Handbook: Approaches to Stress and Trauma*, eds. M. Kent, M. C. Davis and J. W. Reich (New York and London: Routledge) pp 73-85.

Werner, E. E. and Smith, R. S. 1981, *Vulnerable but Invincible: A Longitudinal Study of Resilient Children and Youth*, (New York: McGraw-Hill Book Co).

Williams, J. and Nelson-Gardell, D. 2012, 'Predicting resilience in sexually abused adolescents', *Child Abuse and Neglect*, vol. 36, no. 1, pp 53-63.

Williams, Mark and Penman, Danny, 2011. *Mindfulness: a Practical Guide to Finding Peace in a Frantic World* (London: Piatkus).

Windle, G., Wagnild, G. M. and Collins, J. A. 2009, 'Assessing resilience', *Journal of Psychosocial Nursing and Mental Health Services*, vol. 47, no. 12, pp 28-33.

Wu, G., Feder, A., Cohen, H., Kim, J. J., Calderon, S., Charney, D. S. and Mathé, A. A. 2013, 'Understanding resilience', *Frontiers in Behavioral Neuroscience*, vol. 7, pp 10-25.

Yates, T. M. and Masten, A. S., 2004. 'Fostering the future: resilience theory and the practice of positive psychology', in *Positive Psychology in Practice*, eds. P. A. Linley and S. Joseph (Hoboken, NJ: Wiley) pp 521-539.

Zautra, A. J., Hall, J. S. and Murray, K. E. 2010, 'Resilience: a new definition of health for people and communities' in *Handbook of Adult Resilience*, eds. J. W. Reich, A. J. Zautra and J. S. Hall (New York: Guildford Press) pp 3-29.

If you have enjoyed this book, you might like to consider

- *supporting the work of the Latimer Trust*
- *reading more of our publications*
- *recommending them to others*

See www.latimertrust.org for more information.

Latimer Publications

	Latimer Studies	
LS 01	*The Evangelical Anglican Identity Problem*	Jim Packer
LS 02	*The ASB Rite A Communion: A Way Forward*	Roger Beckwith
LS 03	*The Doctrine of Justification in the Church of England*	Robin Leaver
LS 04	*Justification Today: The Roman Catholic and Anglican Debate*	R. G. England
LS 05/06	*Homosexuals in the Christian Fellowship*	David Atkinson
LS 07	*Nationhood: A Christian Perspective*	O. R. Johnston
LS 08	*Evangelical Anglican Identity: Problems and Prospects*	Tom Wright
LS 09	*Confessing the Faith in the Church of England Today*	Roger Beckwith
LS 10	*A Kind of Noah's Ark? The Anglican Commitment to Comprehensiveness*	Jim Packer
LS 11	*Sickness and Healing in the Church*	Donald Allister
LS 12	*Rome and Reformation Today: How Luther Speaks to the New Situation*	James Atkinson
LS 13	*Music as Preaching: Bach, Passions and Music in Worship*	Robin Leaver
LS 14	*Jesus Through Other Eyes: Christology in a Multi-faith Context*	Christopher Lamb
LS 15	*Church and State Under God*	James Atkinson,
LS 16	*Language and Liturgy*	Gerald Bray, Steve Wilcockson, Robin Leaver
LS 17	*Christianity and Judaism: New Understanding, New Relationship*	James Atkinson
LS 18	*Sacraments and Ministry in Ecumenical Perspective*	Gerald Bray
LS 19	*The Functions of a National Church*	Max Warren
LS19_2	*British Values and the National Church: Essays on Church and State from 1964-2014*	ed. David Holloway
LS 20/21	*The Thirty-Nine Articles: Their Place and Use Today*	Jim Packer, Roger Beckwith
LS 22	*How We Got Our Prayer Book*	T.W. Drury, Roger Beckwith
LS 23/24	*Creation or Evolution: a False Antithesis?*	Mike Poole, Gordon Wenham
LS 25	*Christianity and the Craft*	Gerard Moate
LS 26	*ARCIC II and Justification*	Alister McGrath
LS 27	*The Challenge of the Housechurches*	Tony Higton, Gilbert Kirby
LS 28	*Communion for Children? The Current Debate*	A. A. Langdon
LS 29/30	*Theological Politics*	Nigel Biggar
LS 31	*Eucharistic Consecration in the First Four Centuries and its Implications for Liturgical Reform*	Nigel Scotland
LS 32	*A Christian Theological Language*	Gerald Bray
LS 33	*Mission in Unity: The Bible and Missionary Structures*	Duncan McMann
LS 34	*Stewards of Creation: Environmentalism in the Light of Biblical Teaching*	Lawrence Osborn
LS 35/36	*Mission and Evangelism in Recent Thinking: 1974-1986*	Robert Bashford
LS 37	*Future Patterns of Episcopacy: Reflections in Retirement*	Stuart Blanch
LS 38	*Christian Character: Jeremy Taylor and Christian Ethics Today*	David Scott
LS 39	*Islam: Towards a Christian Assessment*	Hugh Goddard
LS 40	*Liberal Catholicism: Charles Gore and the Question of Authority*	G. F. Grimes
LS 41/42	*The Christian Message in a Multi-faith Society*	Colin Chapman
LS 43	*The Way of Holiness 1: Principles*	D. A. Ousley
LS 44/45	*The Lambeth Articles*	V. C. Miller
LS 46	*The Way of Holiness 2: Issues*	D. A. Ousley

Latimer Publications

LS 47	*Building Multi-Racial Churches*	John Root
LS 48	*Episcopal Oversight: A Case for Reform*	David Holloway
LS 49	*Euthanasia: A Christian Evaluation*	Henk Jochemsen
LS 50/51	*The Rough Places Plain: AEA 1995*	
LS 52	*A Critique of Spirituality*	John Pearce
LS 53/54	*The Toronto Blessing*	Martyn Percy
LS 55	*The Theology of Rowan Williams*	Garry Williams
LS 56/57	*Reforming Forwards? The Process of Reception and the Consecration of Woman as Bishops*	Peter Toon
LS 58	*The Oath of Canonical Obedience*	Gerald Bray
LS 59	*The Parish System: The Same Yesterday, Today And For Ever?*	Mark Burkill
LS 60	*'I Absolve You': Private Confession and the Church of England*	Andrew Atherstone
LS 61	*The Water and the Wine: A Contribution to the Debate on Children and Holy Communion*	Roger Beckwith, Andrew Daunton-Fear
LS 62	*Must God Punish Sin?*	Ben Cooper
LS 63	*Too Big For Words? The Transcendence of God and Finite Human Speech*	Mark D. Thompson
LS 64	*A Step Too Far: An Evangelical Critique of Christian Mysticism*	Marian Raikes
LS 65	*The New Testament and Slavery: Approaches and Implications*	Mark Meynell
LS 66	*The Tragedy of 1662: The Ejection and Persecution of the Puritans*	Lee Gatiss
LS 67	*Heresy, Schism & Apostasy*	Gerald Bray
LS 68	*Paul in 3D: Preaching Paul as Pastor, Story-teller and Sage*	Ben Cooper
LS69	*Christianity and the Tolerance of Liberalism: J.Gresham Machen and the Presbyterian Controversy of 1922-1937*	Lee Gatiss
LS70	*An Anglican Evangelical Identity Crisis: The Churchman–Anvil Affair of 1981-4*	Andrew Atherstone
LS71	*Empty and Evil: The worship of other faiths in 1 Corinthians 8-10 and today*	Rohintan Mody
LS72	*To Plough or to Preach: Mission Strategies in New Zealand during the 1820s*	Malcolm Falloon
LS73	*Plastic People: How Queer Theory is Changing Us*	Peter Sanlon
LS74	*Deification and Union with Christ: Salvation in Orthodox and Reformed thought*	Slavko Eždenci
LS75	*As It Is Written: Interpreting the Bible with Boldness*	Benjamin Sargent
LS76	*Light From Dark Ages? An Evangelical Critique of Celtic Spirituality*	Marian Raikes
LS77	*The Ethics of Usury*	Ben Cooper
LS78	*For Us and For Our Salvation: 'Limited Atonement' in the Bible, Doctrine, History and Ministry*	Lee Gatiss
LS79	*Positive Complementarianism: The Key Biblical Texts*	Ben Cooper
LS80	*Were they Preaching 'Another Gospel'? Justification by Faith in the Second Century*	Andrew Daunton-Fear
LS81	*Thinking Aloud: Responding to the Contemporary Debate about Marriage, Sexuality and Reconciliation*	Martin Davie
LS82	*Spells, Sorcerers and Spirits: Magic and the Occult in the Bible*	Kirsten Birkett
LS83	*Your Will Be Done: Exploring Eternal Subordination, Divine Monarchy and Divine Humility*	Michael J Ovey
LS84	*Resilience: A Spiritual Project*	Kirsten Birkett

LATIMER PUBLICATIONS

	Latimer Briefings	
LB01	*The Church of England: What it is, and what it stands for*	R. T. Beckwith
LB02	*Praying with Understanding: Explanations of Words and Passages in the Book of Common Prayer*	R. T. Beckwith
LB03	*The Failure of the Church of England? The Church, the Nation and the Anglican Communion*	A. Pollard
LB04	*Towards a Heritage Renewed*	H.R.M. Craig
LB05	*Christ's Gospel to the Nations: The Heart & Mind of Evangelicalism Past, Present & Future*	Peter Jensen
LB06	*Passion for the Gospel: Hugh Latimer (1485–1555) Then and Now. A commemorative lecture to mark the 450th anniversary of his martyrdom in Oxford*	A. McGrath
LB07	*Truth and Unity in Christian Fellowship*	Michael Nazir-Ali
LB08	*Unworthy Ministers: Donatism and Discipline Today*	Mark Burkill
LB09	*Witnessing to Western Muslims: A Worldview Approach to Sharing Faith*	Richard Shumack
LB10	*Scarf or Stole at Ordination? A Plea for the Evangelical Conscience*	Andrew Atherstone
LB11	*How to Write a Theology Essay*	Michael P. Jensen
LB12	*Preaching: A Guidebook for Beginners*	Allan Chapple
LB13	*Justification by Faith: Orientating the Church's teaching and practice to Christ (Toon Lecture 1)*	Michael Nazir-Ali
LB14	*"Remember Your Leaders": Principles and Priorities for Leaders from Hebrews 13*	Wallace Benn
LB15	*How the Anglican Communion came to be and where it is going*	Michael Nazir-Ali
LB16	*Divine Allurement: Cranmer's Comfortable Words*	Ashley Null
LB17	*True Devotion: In Search of Authentic Spirituality*	Allan Chapple
LB18	*Commemorating War & Praying for Peace: A Christian Reflection on the Armed Forced*	John Neal

	Anglican Foundations Series	
FWC	*The Faith We Confess: An Exposition of the 39 Articles*	Gerald Bray
AF02	*The 'Very Pure Word of God': The Book of Common Prayer as a Model of Biblical Liturgy*	Peter Adam
AF03	*Dearly Beloved: Building God's People Through Morning and Evening Prayer*	Mark Burkill
AF04	*Day by Day: The Rhythm of the Bible in the Book of Common Prayer*	Benjamin Sargent
AF05	*The Supper: Cranmer and Communion*	Nigel Scotland
AF06	*A Fruitful Exhortation: A Guide to the Homilies*	Gerald Bray
AF07	*Instruction in the Way of the Lord: A Guide to the Prayer Book Catechism*	Martin Davie
AF08	*Till Death Us Do Part: "The Solemnization of Matrimony" in the Book of Common Prayer*	Simon Vibert
AF09	*Sure and Certain Hope: Death and Burial in the Book of Common Prayer*	Andrew Cinnamond

Latimer Publications

Latimer Books

Code	Title	Author/Editor
GGC	*God, Gays and the Church: Human Sexuality and Experience in Christian Thinking*	eds. Lisa Nolland, Chris Sugden, Sarah Finch
WTL	*The Way, the Truth and the Life: Theological Resources for a Pilgrimage to a Global Anglican Future*	eds. Vinay Samuel, Chris Sugden, Sarah Finch
AEID	*Anglican Evangelical Identity – Yesterday and Today*	J.I.Packer, N.T.Wright
IB	*The Anglican Evangelical Doctrine of Infant Baptism*	John Stott, Alec Motyer
BF	*Being Faithful: The Shape of Historic Anglicanism Today*	Theological Resource Group of GAFCON
TPG	*The True Profession of the Gospel: Augustus Toplady and Reclaiming our Reformed Foundations*	Lee Gatiss
SG	*Shadow Gospel: Rowan Williams and the Anglican Communion Crisis*	Charles Raven
TTB	*Translating the Bible: From William Tyndale to King James*	Gerald Bray
PWS	*Pilgrims, Warriors, and Servants: Puritan Wisdom for Today's Church*	ed. Lee Gatiss
PPA	*Preachers, Pastors, and Ambassadors: Puritan Wisdom for Today's Church*	ed. Lee Gatiss
CWP	*The Church, Women Bishops and Provision: The Integrity of Orthodox Objections to the Proposed Legislation Allowing Women Bishops*	
TSF	*The Truth Shall Set You Free: Global Anglicans in the 21st Century*	ed. Charles Raven
LMM	*Launching Marsden's Mission: The Beginnings of the Church Missionary Society in New Zealand, viewed from New South Wales*	eds. Peter G Bolt, David B. Pettett
MST1	*Listen To Him: Reading and Preaching Emmanuel in Matthew*	ed. Peter G Bolt
MLD1	*From Cambridge to Colony: Charles Simeon's Enduring Influence on Christianity in Australia*	ed. Edward Loane
GWC	*The Genius of George Whitefield: Reflections on his Ministry from 21st Century Africa*	eds. Benjamin Dean, Adriaan Neele
MST2	*'Tend My Sheep': The word of God and pastoral ministry*	ed. Keith G Condie

Lightning Source UK Ltd.
Milton Keynes UK
UKOW01f0731180810

280966UK00002B/81/P